Collectio Toletana

A Canon Law Derivative of the South-Italian *Collection in Five Books*

DOUGLAS ADAMSON *and* ROGER E. REYNOLDS

This book contains a study and a critical implicit or incipit-explicit edition of an eleventh-century canon law collection based on two important major canonical collections of the eleventh century: the *Collection in Five Books* compiled in southern Italy, and the famous *Decretum* of Burchard of Worms that was quickly copied in both southern and central Italy in the eleventh century. The *Collectio Toletana* is one of at least twenty-five derivative collections based on the *Collection in Five Books*, and its length and diversity of canons make it an appropriate subject for a study and critical edition.

Given the critical need for modern editions of the major early canon law collections, scholars have long been urged to channel their energies toward these and not minor and derivative collections found in one or a few codices. The complexities of producing such editions, which have become increasingly apparent over the past few decades, would appear to suggest more modest, circumscribed goals. However, a partial edition of a text such as the one produced here can still be justified on several grounds even though there is no evidence as of yet that the *Collectio Toletana* had any influence on other collections.

First, it is now clear that the *Collection in Five Books* was the most significant indigenous Italian collection of the first half of the eleventh century and continued to exercise great influence in canonistic studies well into the twelfth century, especially in its derivatives, of which the *Collectio Toletana* is one. Second, an edition of its derivatives will be useful in controlling the edition of the *Collection in Five Books*. Third, the light shed by the derivative collections should allow for a more finely tuned reconstruction of the original. And finally, editions and studies of the derivatives, in all their peculiarity and idiosyncracy, will undoubtedly help reveal the existence of manuscripts of the *Collection* and variants thereof that were available in the eleventh century.

Monumenta Liturgica Beneventana

V

STUDIES AND TEXTS 159

Collectio Toletana

A Canon Law Derivative of the South-Italian *Collection in Five Books*

An implicit edition with introductory study

DOUGLAS ADAMSON

and

ROGER E. REYNOLDS

PONTIFICAL INSTITUTE OF MEDIAEVAL STUDIES

Acknowledgement

This book has been published with the help of a grant from the Canadian Federation for the Humanities and Social Sciences, through the Aid to Scholarly Publications Program, using funds provided by the Social Sciences and Humanities Research Council of Canada.

Library and Archives Canada Cataloguing in Publication

Collectio Toletana

Collectio Toletana : a canon law derivative of the South-Italian Collection in five books : an implicit edition with introductory study / Douglas Adamson and Roger E. Reynolds.

(Monumenta liturgica Beneventana ; 5)
(Studies and texts, ISSN 0082-5328 ; 159)
Text in Latin; introduction and notes in English.
Includes bibliographical references and indexes.
ISBN 978-0-88844-159-1

1. Canon law – Early works to 1800. 2. Canon law – History – To 1500. I. Adamson, Douglas II. Reynolds, Roger E., 1936– III. Pontifical Institute of Mediaeval Studies IV. Title. V. Series. VI. Series: Studies and texts (Pontifical Institute of Mediaeval Studies) ; 159

KBR1315.C64 2008 262.909'021 C2008-903572-0

Pontifical Institute of Mediaeval Studies
59 Queen's Park Crescent East
Toronto, Ontario, Canada M5S 2C4

www.pims.ca

MANUFACTURED IN CANADA

Contents

Preface

In the incipit-explicit 'implicit edition' published some years ago of the canon law collection found in the manuscript Montecassino Archivio della Badia 216, I indicated that a similar edition of another canon law collection based on the south-Italian *Collection in Five Books* might be released soon.[1] This is the *Collectio Toletana*, here edited with an introductory study. Although this collection had been known since the announcement of its existence by Antonio García y García in 1965,[2] the first extensive work on the collection was carried out by John Douglas Adamson in his 1987 report for the M.S.L. degree awarded by the Pontifical Institute of Mediaeval Studies in Toronto.[3]

After completing this study, Douglas Adamson began work for the PhD degree in the Centre for Medieval Studies at the University of Toronto. Rather than continuing his study of early medieval canon law collections, he chose to edit and study a medieval commentary on Roman law by Placentinus.[4] Many scholars asked him to publish these two editions, but by this time Dr Adamson had embarked on a different career.

The Pontifical Institute and the University of Toronto still receive inquiries about his editions of the *Collectio Toletana* and the *Summa Institutionum* of Placentinus, but since his interests have now turned in other directions, Dr Adamson has generously offered his collaboration in the preparation of an implicit edition of the *Collectio Toletana*. Because this collection is one of the derivatives of the south-Italian

1 Roger E. Reynolds, *The Collectio canonum Casinensis duodecimi seculi (Codex terscriptus): A Derivative of the South-Italian* Collection in Five Books: *An Implicit Edition with Introductory Study*, Monumenta Liturgica Beneventana 3, Studies and Texts 137 (Toronto: Pontifical Institute of Mediaeval Studies, 2001), ix.

2 Antonio García y García, "Los manuscritos jurídicos medievales de la Catedral de Toledo," *Traditio* 21 (1965) 511–512; and "Canonistica Hispanica (II)," *Traditio* 23 (1967) 504–511.

3 John Douglas Adamson, "The *Collectio Toletana*" (M.S.L. Report, Pontifical Institute of Mediaeval Studies, Toronto, 1987).

4 John Douglas Adamson, "A Critical Edition of the *Summa Institutionum* of Placentinus" (PhD dissertation, University of Toronto, 1991).

canonical collections that have been one of the focuses of the Monumenta Liturgica Beneventana at the Pontifical Institute, it was decided to prepare an 'implicit' edition like that of the Collectio canonum Casinensis of Montecassino 216, with grateful acknowledgement of the original work of Douglas Adamson.

Beyond Dr Adamson this study and edition owes debts of thanks to many institutions and colleagues: the Social Sciences and Humanities Council of Canada for financial support of the program Monumenta Liturgica Beneventana, the Pontifical Institute of Mediaeval Studies, Don Ramón Gonzálvez-Ruíz, the emeritus archivist of the Archivio y Biblioteca Capitular of Toledo, Don Faustino Avagliano, the archivist and prior of the abbey of Montecassino, Professor Virginia Brown, Dr Linda Fowler-Magerl, and for their friendly support along the way Professor Maria Crescenza Carrocci and her greater family, Professor James Hankins, Vittorio and Leda D'Errico, Fernando and Lidia Miele, Professor Don Mario Iadanza, Professor Lina Massa, and Lioubov Alexeevna Ivanitskaia.

Introduction

The *Collectio canonum in V Libris* (hereafter 5L) has long been recognized as one of the richest patristic, penitential, and liturgical florilegia circulating in Italy in the half century or so preceding the Gregorian Reform movement of the late eleventh century. Compilers frequently made new collections of extracts from it or combined extracts with other material throughout the Reform period and into the twelfth century. This wide range of influence was first noted by Paul Fournier in 1899 and again in greater detail in 1915[1] and has been steadily confirmed by subsequent scholarship. Twenty-five derivatives are now known.[2]

One of the most interesting features of these derivative texts is how compatible the 5L was with a wide variety of material: the *Corrector sive Medicus* of Burchard of Worms, liturgical material, the *Collection in 74 Titles,* and groups of patristic texts. The 5L and the *Corrector,* particularly, seem to have had a mutual affinity not merely because they were both penitential in character, but also because they were complementary; that is, the 5L had early Greek patristic material not available in other Latin sources as well as a wide range of conciliar, synodal, and other authoritative texts, while the *Corrector* gave an explicit list of sins together with a clear statement of penalties.[3] The fact that there

1 See Paul Fournier, "De l'influence de la Collection Irlandaise sur la formation des collections canoniques," *Revue historique de droit français et étranger*, 4e sér. 23 (1899) 27–78, repr. in *Mélanges de droit canonique,* ed. Theo Kölzer, 2 vols. (Aalen: Scientia Verlag, 1983), 2: 93–144; and also "Un groupe de recueils canoniques italiens des Xe et XIe siècles," *Mémoires de l'Académie des Inscriptions et Belles-Lettres* 40 (1915) 95–213, at 99.

2 On these collections and the material they cover, see Roger E. Reynolds, "The South-Italian Canon Law Collection in Five Books and Its Derivatives: New Evidence on Its Origins, Diffusion, and Use," *Mediaeval Studies* 52 (1990) 278–95.

3 On the *Corrector* see PL 140: 951–976; on *Corrector sive Medicus* (Book XIX) see Hermann Wasserschleben, *Die Bußordnungen der abendländischen Kirche*

are only three known complete or near-complete manuscripts of the 5L[4] compared with twenty-five derivative texts shows the 5L to have been considered more useful in combination than alone. The *Collectio Toletana* edited here is a good example of how the 5L took on a utility when combined with the *Corrector* that makes the derivative collection the vade mecum the 5L never was in its own right. The repairs to the top outside corners of many folios show how the parchment has been worn away by frequent thumbing and demonstrate how useful it was over the years. Further, the components from the 5L have been reduced to practical essentials by the omission of all prefaces and internal divisions found in manuscripts of the 5L. This was clearly a handbook in regular use.

The collection of canons, here designated as the *Collectio Toletana* (hereafter CT) after its place of preservation, was first brought to the attention of modern scholars by Antonio García y García in 1965 and again in more detail in 1967. He observed in the latter article that the eleventh-century manuscript, 22–32 of the Fondo Zelada of the

(1851; repr. Graz: Akademische Druck- u. Verlagsanstalt, 1958), pp. 624–682; Hermann Joseph Schmitz, *Die Bußbücher und die Bußdisciplin der Kirche*, 2 vols. (1883–1898; repr. Graz: Akademische Druck- u. Verlagsanstalt, 1958), 2: 403–467; *A pane e acqua: peccati e penitenze nel Medioevo – Il Penitenziale di Burcardo di Worms*, ed. Giorgio Picasso, Giannino Piana, and Giuseppe Motta, and trans. Giuseppe Motta (Novara: Europìa, 1986), which includes an Italian translation of Book XIX of the *Corrector*; Cyrille Vogel, *Le pécheur et la pénitence au moyen âge* (Paris: Éditions du Cerf, 1969), pp. 80–113 (French translation of Book XIX of the *Corrector*) and "Pratiques superstitieuses au début du XIe siècle d'après le Corrector sive Medicus de Burchard, évêque de Worms (965–1025)," *Études de civilisation médiévale (IXe–XIIe siècles): Mélanges offerts à Edmond-René Labande* (Poitiers: C.É.S.C.M., 1974), pp. 751–761.

4 The more complete manuscripts are: Montecassino, Archivio della Badia, 125 (saec. XImed; Montecassino); Roma, Biblioteca Vallicelliana, B.11 (saec. XI, before 1087; Sant' Eutizio in Val Castoriana, near Nursia); and Città del Vaticano, Biblioteca Apostolica Vaticana, Vat. lat. 1339 (saec. XImed; Italy, Santa Maria, Narni). There is also what is likely a fragmentary manuscript, Roma, Biblioteca Vallicelliana R.32 (fol. 50) (saec. XI3/4; middle Italy).

Archivo y Biblioteca Capitulares of the Cathedral of Toledo, which had been catalogued among the theological material, was in fact a rare penitential collection using the *Corrector* and other well-known texts ("Pero no he visto ninguna otra serie homogénea como la que [i.e., the *Corrector*] acabo de indicar").[5] The source of this other series can now be shown to be the 5L.

The 5L, as Mario Fornasari its most recent editor has argued,[6] was compiled sometime after 1014 and perhaps before 1023 in southern Italy on the borderlands between the Latin and Byzantine cultural regions. It contained indigenous materials, including collections in the traditions of the *Collection of Vallicelliana Tom. XVIII* and the *Collection in Nine Books* of Vatican, BAV, Lat. 1349, together with texts such as those of John of Constantinople extracted from unknown Byzantine sources. The presence of insular and continental penitential material, Frankish capitularies, and Greek patristic texts is understandable if the collection is taken as the product of the previous half century or so of contacts between transalpine reformers on pilgrimage to Rome, Montecassino, and the Gargano peninsula and the equally reform-minded followers of the Basilian monks Nilus of Rossano and Sabas, whose new monastic foundations were spreading north into Campania. Such contacts were facilitated by closer relations between Byzantium and the Latins following the marriage of Emperor Otto II and the Byzantine princess Theophano in 972.

The CT also shows the influence of the *Decretum* of Burchard of Worms. In the light of recent textual evidence, it is clear that the *Decretum* was known in Italy in the second quarter of the century, rather than at the beginning of the third as suggested by Otto Meyer,[7] and had

5 Antonio García y García, "Los manuscritos jurídicos medievales de la Catedral de Toledo," *Traditio* 21 (1965) 511–512; and "Canonistica Hispanica (II)," *Traditio* 23 (1967) 504–511.

6 On Fornasari's edition, see Gérard Fransen, "Principes d'édition des collections canoniques," *Revue d'histoire écclésiastique* 66 (1971) 125–36; and Hubert Mordek, "Anzeigen," *Zeitschrift der Savigny-Stiftung für Rechtsgeschichte: Kanonistische Abteilung* 60 (1974) 477–478.

7 Otto Meyer, "Überlieferung und Verbreitung des Dekrets des Bischofs Burchard von Worms," *Zeitschrift der Savigny-Stiftung für Rechtsgeschichte:*

a favourable reception instead of a "ripudio pressocche completo" as argued by Carlo Guido Mor.[8] The usefulness of Burchard's *Decretum* was quickly recognized. A colophon in one of the oldest manuscripts (Freiburg im Breisgau, Universitätsbibliothek Ms. 7)[9] praises its power to settle synodal disputes "e quibus emergi non est facile absque huius libri auctoritate." The work was also soon found to be a useful aid in curial judgments and canonical instruction, and it quickly arrived in Italy where a "liber canonum Burchardi episcopi" is known to have been in the library of the monastery of San Silvestro at Nonantola near Modena, where it is listed among the forty items acquired by Abbot Rudolph I between 1002 and 1035.[10] Before 1050 the *Decretum* was used by Peter Damian[11] and by 1100 the collection would reach almost all the centres of religious life in Italy.

The *Collectio toletana* bears the imprint of both these sources. Of the 382 canons of the CT, 240 are from the 5L. By far the greatest number (110) come from book 4; book 3 provides 49, book 5 contributes 47, and book 2 is the source for 34. Only one canon of the CT, the *Ordo defunctorum* from the Pseudo-Alcuinian *Liber de divinis officiis* (CT 180), cannot be found in the 5L or Burchard. Burchard's *Decretum* supplies 142 canons, of which 135 are from the *Corrector*. These facts suggest that the CT was based on a now lost codex containing a version of the 5L somewhat different from those of the three extant manuscripts.

Kanonistische Abteilung 24 (1935) 141–183.

8 Carlo Guido Mor, "La reazione al *Decretum Burchardi* in Italia avanti la Riforma Gregoriana," *Studi Gregoriani* 1 (1947) 197–206.

9 Freiburg i. Breisgau, Universitätsbibliothek, 7 (saec. XI: 1034x1046; Constance), fol. 311v. For the complete text of this colophon, see Meyer, "Überlieferung und Verbreitung," 153 n2.

10 See Roger E. Reynolds, *The Collectio canonum Casinensis duodecimi seculi (Codex terscriptus): A Derivative of the South-Italian* Collection in Five Books*: An Implicit Edition with Introductory Study,* Monumenta Liturgica Beneventana 3, Studies and Texts 137 (Toronto: Pontifical Institute of Mediaeval Studies, 2001), p. 1.

11 Ibid., p. 2.

When the compiler of the CT arranged his canons he did not follow the sequence of the 5L throughout. The first thirty-two begin in the latter part of book 3 of the 5L and run through to the middle of book 4, where suddenly two canons on homosexuality from book 5 are inserted into a group dealing with theft. The sequence continues through book 4 until near the end of book 5, where seven canons from Burchard's *Decretum* book 9 and one from his *Corrector* appear. After reaching the end of book 5 of the 5L our compiler returns to books 2 and 3 and follows the order of the 5L (CT 119–180) before inserting an *Ordo defunctorum*. He then picks up the sequence of book 3 of the 5L again for another four canons before adding a block of 134 canons from the *Corrector*. The Pseudo-Hieronymian-Damasus correspondence and Mass commentary (CT 320)[12] is then added out of order before the sequence resumes through book 4 (CT 321–334). Three canons are then inserted from earlier in book 4 (CT 335–337). The sequence from book 4 then resumes and continues uninterrupted until CT 361 where 3.279 in Fornasari's edition (CT 1) is repeated. More canons from book 4 follow down to CT 376, where three canons from book 2 are added at CT 377–379 and the collection is then completed by three canons from book 5 of the 5L.

A comparison of every twentieth canon of the CT with the three manuscripts of the 5L shows either no variants or insignificant differences such as "omnibus diebus" for "diebus omnibus" (CT 337). Canon 20 is in the singular in our collection and in the plural in the other three manuscripts.

The overall character of the CT is clearly penitential. The complete absence of canons from book 1 of the 5L shows our compiler to have been little interested in matters of ecclesiastical administration. He is chiefly concerned with the nature of penance, sexual offenses of various types, oaths and perjury, murder and manslaughter, fasting, theft, baptism, tithes, and pagan superstitions. Many canons refer specifically

12 See Roger E. Reynolds, "A South Italian Liturgico-Canonical Mass Commentary," *Mediaeval Studies* 50 (1988) 626–670.

to the conduct of clerics and a few, such as 145ff., are directed to monks. In our collection, canon 147 begins "Si quis abbas ..." as it does in Rome, Biblioteca Vallicelliana, B 11, fol. 95r and in Montecassino, Archivio della Badia, Cod. 125 (hereafter C), p. 115, both of which were written in monastic settings. In Vatican, BAV, Vat. lat. 1339 (hereafter V), fol. 102va, it reads "Si quis episcopus vel abbas ..." and at fol. 122ra "Si quis episcopus ... ." The fact that the CT contains the "Si quis abbas" version grouped with other canons on monastic behavior suggests an intention to direct the collection to monastic use. The mixed character of the collection, however, indicates that it was probably compiled for the self-regulation of clerics and monks as well as the shriving of lay penitents.

As for the recensions of the 5L used by the compiler of CT, he generally follows a text like that of V. Indeed, in some cases, such as canons 96 and 355f., V contains these texts, whereas C does not. On the other hand, at times the compiler used a source closer to C than to V. For example, the ending of canon 104 corresponds to the text in C, not V. The sequence of canons from the 5L followed by CT is at times closer to V than C. For example, in canons 151–154 the compiler draws from 3.44 to 3.47 in V, but in C this sequence is 3.30 to 3.28, or in canons 327–329 the sequence follows V, canons 112, 113, 114, not C, canons 81, 80, 69. In canon 361 the compiler of CT followed the conclusion of the text in V, f. 201va, but attributed the canon to a Council of Tarragona, perhaps because he had attributed the preceding canon to this same council. In short, the compiler of CT generally followed a text closer to V than to C, but at times his text is closer to this latter manuscript.

In his summary of work in progress in the edition of early medieval canon law collections in the 1950s, the late Mgr. J.J. Ryan of the Pontifical Institute of Mediaeval Studies stated that given the critical need for modern editions of the major early collections, scholars should channel their energies toward these and not minor and derivative collections found in one or a few codices.[13] Since the time of Ryan's article, the need for modern critical editions of collections is no less desir-

13 See Reynolds, *Collectio canonum Casinensis*, p. vii.

able. But the complexities of producing such editions have subsequently been stressed by scholars in their preliminary work on the major collections.[14] Hence, it might be argued that scholars should "scale down" their sights and begin to produce editions, either full or partial, of the more minor collections. A partial edition of a text such as the one produced here can be justified on several grounds even though there is no evidence as of yet that the CT had any influence on other collections. First, it is now clear that the 5L was the most significant indigenous Italian collection of the first half of the eleventh century and continued to exercise great influence in canonistic studies well into the twelfth century, especially in its derivatives, of which the CT is one. Second, an edition of the derivatives of the 5L will be useful in controlling the edition of the 5L itself and other derivatives. There are, as has been pointed out, only three manuscripts extant of the 5L, none of which is a copy of the others and all of which are significantly different in the numbers of texts they contain and even in the recensions of individual texts. Moreover, it is known that a number of manuscripts of the collections have disappeared.[15] Hence, the light that the derivative collections can shed on the original 5L and its reconstruction is important indeed. And finally, editions and studies of the derivatives of the 5L, with their own peculiarities, will undoubtedly help reveal the existence of manuscripts of the 5L and variants thereof available in the eleventh century.

14 See Horst Fuhrmann, "Kanonistische Konzilsüberlieferung und Archetyp: Zur Qualität von Burchardtexten," in *Proceedings of the Eighth International Congress of Medieval Canon Law*, ed. Stanley Chodorow, Monumenta Iuris Canonici, Series C: Subsidia 9 (Vatican City: Biblioteca Apostolica Vaticana, 1991), pp. 57–62; the reviews of Fornasari's edition cited in n6 above; as well as Hartmut Hoffmann and Rudolf Pokorny, *Das Dekret des Bischofs Burchard von Worms: Textstufen, frühe Verbreitung, Vorlagen,* Monumenta Germaniae Historica: Hilfsmittel 12 (Munich: MGH, 1991).

15 See, for example, the comments of Theo Kölzer on the 5L source for the *Collectio Farfensis* in *Collectio canonum Regesto Farfensi inserta*, ed. Theo Kölzer, Monumenta Iuris Canonici, Series B: Corpus collectionum 5 (Vatican City: Biblioteca Apostolica Vaticana, 1982), pp. 50–55.

Codicological and Paleographical Features of the Toledo Manuscript

BINDING. The manuscript, Toledo, Catedral, Archivo y Biblioteca Capitulares 22–32, is a small volume bound in red leather covers 185 x 105 mm with a gold-tooled border on the front cover. Between the first and second of the spine's five ribs is the title "Canones Poenitent." Near the bottom of the spine are Cardinal Zelada's family coat of arms and his initials. There are no designs on the back cover and no ties or clasps of any kind.

END-PAPERS AND FLY LEAVES. Marbled end-papers are glued to the inside front and back covers. The front paper bears the cardinal's emblem with the Zelada coat of arms inset. Since Zelada was made cardinal in 1773, the presence of the cardinal's emblem shows that the manuscript was probably bound sometime after this date. There are two fly-leaves at the front and two at the back. On the recto of the second front fly-leaf are the words "Ca fon 22 Num 32 Zelada."

PAGINATION. The manuscript is paginated 1–255 with page 40 numbered as 79 on both recto and verso.

NOTAE POSSESSORIS. A *nota possessoris,* "F. Mauritii Tertii," appears at the top of p. 1 written in a modern hand. This might possibly be a frater in the Augustinian convent of the Most Holy Trinity at Viterbo since written in a different modern hand at the bottom of the page around a hole that was later repaired are the words: "Viterbii a me cum essem Monasterii Sanctissimae Trinitatis prior anno m.d.xxciil [sic] inter abiecta quedam folia inventus Canonum Poenitentialium Liber" (the date should perhaps read "mdxxciij'). Whether these discarded leaves and penitential book were found in the convent itself by its prior is uncertain. Nor is it clear how the manuscript came into the hands of Cardinal Zelada nearly two centuries later.

CONDITION. Repairs are evident throughout, most having been done at the corners with the page numbers written over the repairs. There is the repaired hole on p. 1 and an un-repaired hole on p. 68. Pages 2 and 3 are heavily stained with red ink. Page 255 has a series of intruded biblical quotations (Lam 1.1; Mt 24.45; Judith 7.17) together with some other illegible material running across the top and down the right margin. The hand of these marginalia is different from those of the text, rubrics, and glosses.

COLLATION. Leaves are folded and bound so that hair-side faces hair-side and flesh-side faces flesh-side in sixteen quaternions, except for gathering four, which has two, and gathering five, which has fourteen: hence Q 1^8–3^8, 4^2, 5^{14}, 6^8–16^8. This imbalance reflects the fact that page 26 has been mis-bound after page 321. The page order should thus run: 49, 50, 53, 54, 55, 56, 57, 58, 59, 60, 61, 62, 63, 64, 51, 52, 65, 66, etc. Since the page numbers run consecutively throughout the manuscript and are written on the repaired corners, it seems likely that the manuscript was repaired, bound with page 26 out of order, and then numbered.

PRICKING AND RULING. Prickings are clearly visible on most pages outside the vertical boundary lines. There are twenty-one ruled drypoint horizontal lines per page with the text in a single column in a writing frame 130 x 65mm. The outer margin is 20mm wide, the top 13 mm and the bottom 32mm.

INKS. Titles are in red ink and the text is in black. The first letter of the first word in each canon is written in red, then written over in black and sometimes decorated in the same colours. Throughout the text the black-on-red technique is used for the first letter of a new sentence within a canon. There are no illustrations, miniatures, or decorated initials.

CAPITALS. In some instances rustic capitals are used to begin canons and in others majuscule letters. In places the whole first line is capitalized (e.g., c. 121 page 88); capitalization of only the first word or two (e.g., SI QUIS) is common throughout.

INSTRUCTIONS FOR RUBRICATION. Parts of the instructions to the rubricator can still be read at the outer edge of many pages. Some of these instructions were not carried out. For example, the rubricator entirely omitted the M of MOLLIS and forgot to blacken the S of SI QUIS on page 22. The large lacuna between canons 106 and 107 on page 75 suggests the rubricated title has been omitted. Misspellings in the rubrics are frequent: thus, "maficiis" for the still clearly visible "maleficiis" of the instructions at the bottom of page 233.

GLOSSES. Almost all of the very few glosses, in a contemporary hand, are interlinear and written in red. On page 118, the first part (*id est tertia)* of the gloss above line 1 is in the same ink as the text while the remainder (*vel nona)* is in red. The glosses give simple synonyms for words in the text. A random sampling shows that all glosses in the CT are found in Vat. lat. 1339 but not vice versa. For example, "interdum" of c. 165, page 124, is glossed "saepe vel aliquando" in Vat. lat. 1339, but simply "aliquando" in the CT. The word "urgeatur" of canon 122, page 90, is glossed by "compellatur vel praeoccupatur" in both Vat. lat. 1339 and Montecassino 125 but only by "compellatur" in the CT. These words are not glossed in Vallicelliana B 11.

SCRIBAL HANDS. The manuscript is written by two hands. The first hand copied pages 1–160, the last 16 lines of pages 161 and the first 12 of page 162, all of pages 163–164 and 170–172, the last eighteen lines of page 174, and all of page 175. The second hand was responsible for the remainder.

SCRIPTS. The script of the codex is Carolingian minuscule, resembling romanesca,[16] and not highly abbreviated; where abbreviations occur they frequently indicate Beneventan influences, as noted below. The simultaneous use of minuscule and majuscule "n" is common; e.g., "noN" (page 17.12). Majuscule "T" is frequently found at the end of a plural verb, as in "fueriNT" (page 1.8). Majuscule ligature "NT" is found in "obedieNT" (page 36.3). The Carolingian minuscule and majuscule "r" can be seen together in "separentuR" (page 110.8). The insular "est" sign X with two dots is to be found throughout especially as the auxili-

16 Virginia Brown, who has seen photos of some of the folios, has observed that there is a certain romanesca cast to the script of the Toledo manuscript, i.e., the small, high loop of e, small shoulder of r, broad cross-stroke of t, and medial i with a small stroke to the right (at the top) and a small stroke to the left (at the bottom). There is often a rightward lean to the entire script as well. But since the rightward lean is not always there, perhaps this is an example of romanesca written on the periphery of the romanesca zone.

ary in the perfect passive form of the verb; e.g., "ductu" X" (page 43.18). It represents "es" in "coinquinatus es" (page 179.15). The unusual Irish "p" for "pro" appears on page 120.16 and many other places. The Carolingian and Beneventan "et" sign "&" is used throughout (as it is in other scripts), and the insular "7" is also present, as on page 3 line 7.

BENEVENTAN INFLUENCE. The Beneventan influence is important for dating the manuscript. The characteristic Beneventan "c" for "con" is used instead of the tyronian '. The Beneventan ' to represent both "s" and "us" is present throughout the text and is used once (page 50 line 15) for "as." E.A. Loew notes that this symbol, while not found before the eleventh century, "is already freely employed"[17] in Monte Cassino 125, one of the three known manuscripts of the 5L and attributed by many scholars to the time of Abbot Theobald (1022–35) but more likely to the middle of the eleventh century. The abbreviations for the case-forms of "omnis" are also useful for dating Beneventan manuscripts since they start to change about the middle of the eleventh century from the mere omission of "n" to the omission of "mn," i.e., from "omis" to "ois."[18] In the CT, both forms are used by each hand, e.g., pages 7 line 5; 15 line 10; 217 line 2; 232 line 10.

The presence of these forms and their consistent use by both scribal hands, together with the fact that the manuscript could have been written only after the completion and dissemination of both Burchard's *Decretum* and the 5L, strengthens the suggestion that the CT was copied in central Italy about the middle of the eleventh century. The fact that the *nota possessoris* on page 1 mentions Viterbo further strengthens the possibility of a central Italian origin for the manuscript. One of the major manuscripts of the 5L, Vatican BAV Vat. lat. 1339 (in romanesca with its

17 E.A. Loew, *The Beneventan Script: A History of the South Italian Minuscule*, 2nd enlarged edition prepared by Virginia Brown, 2 vols., Sussidi eruditi 33–34 (Rome, 1980), 2: 213.

18 Ibid, pp. 211, but Virginia Brown notes that this criterion should be used with caution since some very late liturgical manuscripts in Beneventan script use the early form.

Beneventan features), was copied in central Italy, as were several other of its derivatives, and hence it is not surprising to find the CT there also.[19]

Editorial Principles

In Douglas Adamson's licentiate thesis texts were often presented with very short incipits and explicits, but here, following the work of Dr Fowler-Magerl,[20] all canons are presented with both incipit and explicit of at least six words. In his licentiate thesis the classically trained Dr Adamson often classicized the medieval orthography, but following the recommendation of Paul Meyvaert,[21] the spellings of CT, as a medieval text, have been retained throughout here. Where there are omissions or the text is ungrammatical, asyntactical, or unintelligible a short negative apparatus citing the reading in CT has been provided using V or Vat. lat. 1339 as a base text. Simple misspellings have been corrected in curved brackets. All rubricated words are capitalized. For ease of use the canons are numbered individually here in arabic numerals, despite the fact that: (1) some are not divided in the manuscript into separate paragraphs as are the neighbouring canons, or (2) the "Item" is not rubricated in the manuscript, or (3) two or more parts fall under the same rubricated title.

EXPANSION OF ABBREVIATIONS. Abbreviations have normally been expanded, although when Roman numerals appear in the texts, they have been maintained.

19 On Vatican Vat. lat. 1339 (the 5L) in romanesca see Paola Supino Martini, *Roma e l'area grafica romanesca (secoli X–XII)*, Biblioteca di Scrittura e civiltà 1 (Alessandria: Edizioni dell'orso, 1987), p. 41. Supino Martini would say that cities such as Viterbo, Sutri, and others were on the periphery of the romanesca zone, but she makes no mention of our Toledo manuscript.

20 Linda Fowler-Magerl, *Clavis canonum: Selected Canon Law Collections before 1140: access with data processing*, Monumenta Germaniae Historica, Hilfsmittel 21 (Hanover: Hahn, 2005).

21 See his review of *Vitas sanctorum partum Emeretensium*, ed. A. Maya Sánchez, Corpus Christianorum, Series Latina 116 (Turnhout: Brepols, 1992) in *Speculum* 72 (1997) 526–528.

PRESENTATION OF SOURCES. The sources of those canons deriving from the 5L have been numbered as they are found in Fornasari (F) if they fall within the first three books that he edited; in Vat. lat. 1339 (V); and in Montecassino 125 (C). Canons taken from Burchard's *Decretum* have been numbered according to their divisions in PL 140. In his original licentiate thesis of 1987, Dr Adamson provided a valuable service by listing many of the *fontes materiales* and *fontes formales* for each canon, as did Mario Fornasari in his edition, but this is now unnecessary given such readily available computerized tools as Linda Fowler-Magerl's *Clavis canonum: Selected Canon Law Collections Before 1140*, the *Library of Christian Latin Texts* (*CLCLT*), and the *Patrologia Latina*. Further, for the penitential canons, many of Adamson's citations such as those found in the older works of Schmitz, Wasserschleben, and Finsterwalder have been supplanted by the editions of penitentials by Raymund Kottje in the *Corpus Christianorum, Series Latina*, or the on-going work of the équipe of young scholars at the Rijksuniversiteit Utrecht working under Rob Meens.[22]

22 See Rob Meens, "Penitential Questions: Sin, Satisfaction, and Reconciliation in the Tenth and Eleventh Centuries," *Early Medieval Europe* 14 (2006) 1–6.

Abbreviations

5L	*Collectio canonum in V libris* (*Collection in Five Books*)
Burch.	Burchard, *Decretum* in PL 140
C	Montecassino, Archivio della Badia, Cod. 125
CT	*Collectio Toletana*
F	*Collectio canonum in V libris (lib. i–iii),* ed. Mario Fornasari, Corpus Christianorum Continuatio Mediaevalis 6 (Turnhout: Brepols, 1970)
PL	Patrologiae cursus completus: Series latina, 221 vols. (Paris: Migne, 1844–1864)
V	Vatican, Biblioteca Apostolica Vaticana, Vat. lat. 1339

Collectio Toletana

An Implicit Edition

1. DE NON DAMPNANDIS CLERICIS PER TEMERITATEM. EX CONCILIO LAODICENSI.

Ut non dampnetur aepiscopus in sancta synodo nisi septuaginta duobus testibus nec presbyter nisi xliiii. nec diaconus nisi xxxvii. testimonia.

F. 3.279 (= C. 3.183, p. 168)

2. UT CUM EXCOMMUNICATO NON COMMUNICETUR. CONCILIO NICENO.

Si quis autem quilibet ex clero deprehensi fuerint ... communione tamquam qui regul(am) confidunt aecclesiae.

F. 3.290 (= C. 3.191 p. 169; NB the CT version is an abbreviation of the 5L version.)

3. UT A MALIS HOMINIBUS NON SUSCIPIUNTUR MUNERA.

Synodus Hibernensis decraevit ut sacerdos non accipiat munera iniquorum ... non prodest, tantum huic dona nocent iniqui.

Titulus F. 3.299; textus F. 3.300.1 (= C. 3. 195.1 Titulus, 2 Textus, p. 171; NB the first rubric of C. 3.195 is used with the second part of the canon.)

4. SYNODUS (F)ERVENSIS.

Dona iniquorum quae reprobantur a Deo repro|p. 2|bantur a sanctis.

F. 3.300.2 (= C. 3.195.2, p. 171)

5. Item synodus.

Eorum qui pauperes premunt dona a sacerodotibus refutantur.

F. 3.300.3 (= C. 3.195.2, p. 171)

6. Synodus Romana.

De oblationibus eorum continent tegimen et alimentum cetera iniquorum reprobat altissimus.

F. 3.300.4 (= C. 3.195.2, p. 171)

7. SINODUS ROMANA.

Si quis super mortuum lugendo comam capiti(s) sui truncaverit xl. dies paenit(eat) aut faciem laniaverit.

F. 3.306.1 (= C. 3.200, p. 172)

8. DE SORTIBUS SANCTORUM. SYNODUS ROMANA.

Si quis sorte(s) sanctorum quas contra rationem ... bona sive pro mala que veniunt.

F. 3.328 (= C. 3.214, p. 181)

9. |p. 3| DE CHRISTIANIS. NON DEBENT QUERERE DIVINOS VEL AUGURIANTES.

Augustinus. Ammoneo vos pariter ut nullus ex vobis caragios ... penitentia ei subvenerit in eternum peribit.

CHRISTIANIS NON DEBENTES T F. 3.330.1 (= C. 3.215.2, p. 181 f.)

10. Augustinus. Qui supradictis malis id est caragiis ... prodidert quandiu in illa observantia sit.

F. 3.330.2 (= C. 3.215.2, p. 182)

11. EX CONCILIO BRACARENSI.

Non liceat Christianis traditiones gentilium observare ... |p. 4| ... Ihesu Christi facite gratias agentes Deo.

F. 3.333.1 (= C. 3.217, p. 182)

12. CONCILIO ANCIRANO.

Qui augurias aut auspicia sive sompnia ... vii. annos peniteat, si vero seculares v.

F. 3.337 (= C. 3.219, p. 183)

13. QUOD MODUM PENITENTIE DEBEMUS COGNOSCERE ET PERPETRATA MALA POST PENITENTIAM NON REPETERE.

Gregorius. Penitentiam agere digne |pp. 5–6| non possumus nisi modum quoque cuiusdam penitentie cognoscamus. ... minimis qui se meminit in maximis deliquisse.

V. 4.44 (f. 173vb) (= C. 4.20, p. 199)

14. DE DISCRETIONE PENITENTIE.

Gregorius. Ponunt canones peccantibus: de quibusdam peccatis iii. annos in penitentiam, unum ex his in pane et aqua ... |pp. 7–8| ... suae non sint in gaudio sed in merore ut caro que leta ira Christi ad culpam, afflicta reducat ad veniam.

V. 4.45 (f. 174ra) (= C. 4.21.1, pp. 199 f.)

15. DE INCREPATIONE CONTRA INDOCTO SACERDOTE.

Gregorius. Predictam discretionem paenitentiae ignorantes indocti sacerdotes nesciunt quid dicant ...|p. 9|... qui penitens veraciter sibi subtraxerit de cibo et potu dandum sit cotidie in haelaemosyna.

V. 4.46 (f. 174rb) (= C. 4.21.2, p. 200)

16. DE FRUCTUOSA ET DIGNA PENITENTIA.

Theodorus aepiscopus. Discant igitur sacerdotes qui aecclesiis Domini ... |pp. 10–12| ... quis scandalizatur et ego non uror.

Titulus V. 4.47.1 (f. 174ra); Textus V. 4.47.2 (f.174rb) (= C. 4.22 Titulus, C. 4.22.2 Textus; pp. 200–201)

17. CONCILIO ARELATENSE.

Penitentiam coniugatis non nisi ex consensu danda(m).

V. 4.54 (f. 176va) (= C. 4.25, p. 202)

18. DE HIS QUI NECESSITATE MORTIS URGENTE PENITENTIAM ET SIMUL VIATICUM PETUNT ET HIS QUI OBMUTESCUNT ANTEQUAM AD EOS SACERDOS ACCEDAT. PAPAE LEONIS.

Ita ergo talium necessitati auxiliandum est ... |p. 13| ... et penitentiae et reconciliationis beneficium consequantur.

V. 4.57 (f. 176vb) (= C. 4.[28].1, p. 203)

19. EX CONCILIO CARTAGENENSE.

Paenitentes neglegentes tardius recipiantur.

V. 4.58.4 (f. 177rb) (= C. 4.[30].2, p. 203)

20. EX EPISTOLA PAPAE LEONIS.

Poenitens qui infirmitate viaticum eucharistiae acceperit non se craedat absolutum sine inpositione si supervixerit.

V. 4.58.5 (f. 177rb) (= C. 4.[30].2, p. 203)

21. ORDO AD PENITENTIAM ACCIPIENDAM ET CONFESSIONEM. REGULA CANONICA.

Haec est ratio penitentis et confessionis nostre ... |p. 14| ... cum bona voluntate aut cum episcopo aut cum priori suo.

V. 4.63 (f. 179rb) (= C. 4.37, p. 205)

22. DICTA BEATI HIERONYMI BONIFACII EPISCOPI.

Comperimus namque in penitentiale scriptum scriptum pro die et ebdomada et anno ... |pp. 15–16| ... eroget in helemosyna(m) sive duos sive tres tamen velud facultas hominis est.

V. 4.75.2 (f. 182vb) (= C. 4.[46].1, p. 208)

23. ITEM.

Si quis ieiunare non potest pro uno anno ... |pp. 17–19| ... non remit(ti)tur ei neque hic neque in futuro.

V. 4.76 (f. 183rb) (= C. 4.[46].2, p. 208)

24. DE HIS (QUI) PENITENTIBUS PASSIM LICENTIAM DEDERI(N)T. KAROLUS.

Ut nullus presbiter aut laicus penitentes invitet vinum bibere ... unum vel duos denarios iusta qualitatem paenitentiae dederit.

V. 4.79 (f. 184rb) (= C. 4.49, p. 209)

25. DE DILATORIBUS. EX CONCILIO HELIBERITANO.

Delator dicitur eo quod detegit quod latebat. Si quis delator extiterit fidelis ... diffinierit post iii. annos accipere communionem.

V. 4.147 (f. 196rb) (= C. 4.92.2, p. 222)

26. |p.20| EX CONCILIO CARTHAGINENSI.

Ut clerici accusatores fratrum excommunicentur ... recipiant eos ad communionem, non ad clerum.

V. 4.148 (f. 196rb) (= C. 4.93.2, p. 223)

27. HIERONYMUS SIMILITER PATERIUS.

Si quis mendacium fecerit per ignorantiam ... causa nocuit iusta nociture providentia sacerdotis peniteat.

V. 4.164 (f. 197vb) (= C 4.98.1, p. 224)

28. SINODUS HIBERNENSIS.

Definimus ut omnis penitens omnia sua relinquat et filios et liber expectat Christum quia omnia dabit necessaria.

V. 4.178 (f. 200va) (= C. 4.105.3.3, p. 227)

29. DE FURTO.

Synodus Brancarensis. Qui vero cupiditate captus fuerit furtum fecerit |p. 21| quod abstulit reddat et annis v. paeniteat.

V. 4.203 (f. 204ra) (= C. 4.122.1, p. 232)

30. DE FURTO ECCLESIE.

Leo episcopus. Si de ministerio sanctae aecclesiae qualecumque ... integrum reddatur et vii. annis peniteat.

V. 4.204.2 (f. 204rb) (= C. 4.122.3, p. 233)

31. ITEM.

Si quis clericus furtum aecclesiae fecerit peregrina ei communion tribuatur, id est tribuatur.

V. 4.206 (f. 204rb) (= C. 4.124.2, p. 233)

32. DE FURTO. IUDICIBUS COMEATU.

Si quis furatus fuerit equos aut boves ... |p. 22| ... iuxta qualita(tem) culpe vel dampni sic iudicetur.

V. 4.211 (f. 204vb) (= C. 4.125.2, p. 233)

33. IUDICIUM COMEANI.

(M)ollis i. anno peniteat cum magni(s) vigiliis et orationibus ... assuaeti iiii. vel amplius ut diximus peniteat.

V. 5.190.2 (f. 299ra) (= C. 5.[95]4, p. 315)

34. DE TURPITUDINE MASSCULO ET FEMINA CUM FEMINA.

Si quis masculum cum masculo fornicatus fuerit non ut sodomite ... si cum alia ii. annis peniteat.

V. 5.190.1 (f. 298vb) (= C. 5.[95].3, p. 315)

35. |p.23| PATERIUS.

Qui in religioso loco furatus fuerit cibum ... si quarto iugi exilio priori peniteat.

iugi]lei T   V. 4.215 (f. 205ra) (= C. 4.127.4, p. 234)

36. DE RESTITUTIONE FURTI. SINODUS ROMANA.

Decrevit sancta synodus: Si quis vult confiteri peccata sua sacerdoti ... |p. 24| ... non possit conveniens ut tempore integro paeniteat.

V. 4.218 (f. 205va) (= C. 4.129, p. 234)

37. THEODORUS.

Si quis aliaena diripit quolibetmodo reddat quadruplum ... similiter qui consecrata aliqua furatus fuerit.

V. 4.219 (f. 205va) (= C. 4.130, p. 234)

38. DE (E)O QUI HOMINEM CAPTIVA(VE)RIT.

Si quis servum aut quemcumque hominem ... |p. 25| ... peniteat, si potuerit ut inpius iudicetur.

V. 4.226.1 (f. 206va) (= C. 4.136, pp. 235 f.)

39. DE IURAMENTIS ET PERIURIIS. INPRIMIS DE CONIURATIONE VEL CONSPIRATIONE. EX CONCILIO CHALCEDENSES.

Coniurationis vel conspirationis crimen ab exteris legibus ... Episcopi aut clerici a gradu proprio penitens abiciatur.

V. 4.226.2 (f. 206vb) (= C. 4.137.1, p. 236)

40. DE CLERICIS PER CREATURA(M) IURANTIBUS. EX CONCILIO CARTHAGINENSI.

Clericum per creaturam iurantem acerrime obiurgandum si perstiterit in vitio excommunicandum.

V. 4.226.3 (f. 206vb) (= C. 4.137.2, p. 236)

41. DE TRIBUS IURAMENTIS |p. 26| QUE SOLVENDA SUNT.

Hieronymus. Tria iuramenta solvenda sunt primum cum quis ... incaute iurat non putans esse peccatum.

V. 4.228.1 (f. 207ra) (= C. 4.139.1, p. 236)

42. Origines.

Alii frustra iurant nec se ipsos adiuvant ... ut melius solvere videantur quam implere.

V. 4.228.2 (f. 207ra) (= C. 4.139.1, p. 236)

43. Sinodus.

Definitio incauta laudabiliter |p. 27| solvenda nec prevaricatio sed est temeritatis emendatio.

Definitione T   V. 4.228.3 (f. 207ra) (= C. 1.139.1, p. 236)

44. In Libro regum.

Saul iuravit Ionathan occidere et non occisus est ... et iuramenta irrita aerunt nec tenebitur obnoxia.

V. 4.228.4 (f.207ra) (= C. 4.139.1, p. 236)

45. SINODUS HIBERNENSE.

Iuramentum filii et filiae nesciente patre, iuramentum servi non permittente domino irrita aerunt.

V. 4.228.5 (f. 207rb) (= C. 4.139.1, p. 236)

46. YSIDORUS.

In malis autem promissis rescinde fidem ... |p. 28| ... fuerit non sit observandum sed magis paenitentiae submittendum.

V. 4.228.6 (f. 207rb) (= C. 4.139.1, p. 236)

47. GREGORIUS.

Quod latenter et per vim et inlicite introductum est nulla debet stabilitate subsistere. Scriptum est enim omnia bona erunt incomparatione peiorum.

V. 4.228.7 (f. 207rb) (= C. 4.139.1, p. 236)

48. QUI SACRAMENTO SE OBLIGANT NE AD PACEM REDEANT. CONCILIO ILERDENSE.

|p. 29| Qui sacramento se obligaverit ut ligans ... ad caritatem vero que operit multitudinem peccatorum celeriter venire festinet.

ILERDENSE] HIRERENSE   V. 4.252 (f. 210rb) (= C. 4.149.1, p. 240)

49. DE SANGUINIS EFFUSIONE. IUDICIUM THEODORI.

Si quis aliquem per iram percusserit et sanguine(m) fuderit ... si presbiter i. annum, si episcopus duo annos |p. 30| peniteat.

sanguine T   V. 4.264.2 (f. 213va) (= C. 4.153.8, p. 243)

50. DE RIXA. IUDICIUM COMMEANI.

Si quis per rixam hictu(m) iactans debilem ac deformem ... Qui vero non habet unde restituat i. anno peniteat.

V. 4.264.3 (f. 213va) (= C. 4.154.1, p. 244)

51. DE PARVULIS PERCUTIENTIBUS IN VICEM. IUDICIUM COMMEANI.

Parvuli si invicem se percutiunt vii, dies paeniteant. Si vero adolescentes xl. dies penitea(n)t.

V. 4.264.4 (f. 213vb) (= C. 4.154.2, p. 244)

52. DE DETRACTIONE ET MURMURATIONE ET INVIDIA. THEODORUS.

Si quis aepiscopus aliquem detra(h)it xv. dies peniteat, presbiter xii., diaconus et monachus x., clerici et laici vii. Qui vero verbositate diligens detrahendo fratri vii. dies |p. 31| tacens paeniteat.

V. 4.266 (f. 214rb) (= C. 4.155.2, p. 244)

53. DE MURMURATIONE.

Si quis murmurationem fecerit separetur et opus eius ... nocuit largiter placeat ei et peniteat iudicio sacerdotis.

V. 4.267 (f. 214rb) (= C. 4.156, p. 244)

54. DE EO (QUI) SUPERBE ARGUIT. THEODORI.

Qui superbe caeteros qualibet despectione arguit ... si iterans c, si tertio abhominabitur.

EO IUDICIUM add. T V. 4.268 (f. 214rb) (= C. 4.157.1, pp. 244 f.)

55. DE DEBITIS REDDENDIS.

Iob. Debitum uniuscuiusque solvi. In libro Regum. Redde debitori tuo. Paulus. Reddite omnibus debita.

cuiusque rep. T V. 4.282.1 (f. 216rb) (= C. 4.162.1, p. 247)

56. SINODUS ROMANA.

Omnis |p. 32| qui fraudat debitum fratris excommunicatus sit ... cum debitum proximi tui non reddi(di)sti.

V. 4.282.4 (f. 216rb) (= C. 4.162.1, p. 247)

57. DE EO QUI PIGNUS VEL (DONUM) DE ORNAMENTIS ECCLESIE ACCEPERIT. REGIS HENRI(CI).

Quicumque aliquid in pignus vel donum acceperit ... sit anathema et quamdium tenet communione privetur.

REGIS DE EO T   HUNRI T   V. 4.283 (f. 216rb) (= C. 4.163.1, p. 247)

58. DE SACERDOTE QUI POST LICITUM CIBUM MISSAS CANTARE PRESUMPSERIT. EX CONCILIO AURASICO.

Si quis sacerdos enormiter post solitum cibum ... |p. 33| ... cum pluribus vigiliis et orationibus atque helemosinis peniteat.

URASICO T   V. 4.328 (f. 223vb) (= C. 4.186, p. 353)

59. DE SOLVENDO IEIUNIUM UTILITATIS CAUSA.

Synodus Romana. Bonum (est) advenientibus fratribus humanit(at)is ac dilectionis ... ieiunium cum fuerit fructibus karitatis consumatum.

V. 4.349 (f. 227rb) (= C. 4.191.10, p. 358)

60. DE INDICTO IEIUNIO.

Gregorius. Si quis contempsit indictum ieiunium contra decreta seniorum xl. dies peniteat.

V. 4.355 (f. 228va) (= C. 4.193.3, p. 359)

61. |p. 34| DE HIS QUI ANTE HORA(M) CANONICAM CIBUM SUMUNT. IUDICIO COMMEANI.

Qui anticipat oram canonicam vel suaviora ceteris sumit gule ... gradum ut dictum est vel aetatem tamen ita peniteat.

sumis T   V. 4.375 (f. 230ra) (= C. 4.[196.3], p. 361)

62. DE HELYMOSINA, DE FURTO AUT RAPINA ET RELIQUA (MALA).

Synodus Hibernensis. Haelemosyna de furto aut rapina aut usura aut spoliis ... |p. 35| ... quam inter propria uti ne et propria illicita fiant.

V. 4.387 (f. 234vb) (= C. 4.175, pp. 252 f.)

63. Item. Haelemosyna agentibus infidelibus luce clarius quis offerentibus in aecclesia non licet recipi.

V. 4.387 (f. 234vb) (= C. 4.175, pp. 253)

64. DE HIS QUI OSPITES NON RECIPIUNT ET MANDATAE EVANGELI(CA) NON IMPLENT. IUDICIUM COMMEANI.

Si quis non implet quo(d)libet eorum pro quibus Dominus ... Quanto tempora sic manserit tanto peniteat.

V. 4.411 (f. 240ra) (= C. 4.217.1, p. 258)

65. |p. 36| DE INOBEDIENTIA, EXCUSATIONE VEL CORRECTIONE. SYNODUS ROMANA.

Si quis inobediens est maneat sine cibo ... tacuit tanto in pane et aqua peniteat.

V. 4.427.1 (f. 242vb) (= C. 4.222.1, p. 262)

66. COMMEANUS.

Si quis peccatum parvum reticuit arguat ... |p. 37| ... quam secreto arguat satisfaciat ei tres dies peniteat.

V. 4.427.2 (f. 242vb) (= C. 4.222.2, p. 262)

67. CLERICI ADULATORES DEGRADENTUR. EX CONCILIO CARTHAGINENSE.

Clericus qui adulationibus et proditionibus vacare deprehenditur, degradetur.

V. 4.434 (f. 243va) (= C. 4. 223.7, pp. 262 f.)

68. UT ALTERIUS DISPONSATA(M) NEMO ACCIPERE PRESUMAT.

Syricus episcopus. Ne quis disponsatam alterius accipiat quia instar sacrilegii ... coniunctio que a sacerdote benedici non potest.

V. 5.9.1 (f. 255va) (= C. 5.7.2, p. 273)

69. THEODORUS EPISCOPUS.

Disponsatam non licet parentibus tradere altero viro ... tamen in monasterium licebit ire si volu|p. 38|erint.

V. 5.9.2 (f. 255va) (= C. 5.7.2, p. 273)

70. DE PARENTIBUS (QUI FIDEM) SPONSALIORUM FRANGUNT.

Si quis parentes fidem fregerint sponsalium ... crimine fuerint deprehensi excusati erunt parentes.

V. 5.12 (f. 256ra) (= C. 5.8.7, pp. 273 f.)

71. DE DISPONSATIS PUELLIS ET AB ALIIS RAPTIS VEL CORRUPTIS. CONCILIO ANCIRANO.

Disponsata(s) puellas et post ab aliis raptas ... eis a raptoribus vis inlata constiterit.

V. 5.13 (f. 256rb) (= C. 5.14.1, p. 274)

72. DE PUELLIS RAPTIS NECDUM DISPO(N)SATIS VEL MULIERIBUS. CONCILIO CALCEDONENSE.

De his qui rapiunt puellas aut mulieres ... |p. 39| ... legitima rapta sibi iurae coniungere nullatenus possint.

4 inrae T V. 5.19 (f. 257ra) (= C. 5.[16].1, pp. 274 f).

73. DE RAPTURA. IUDICIUM COMMEANI.

Si quis virginem vel viduam rapuerit v. annos cum pane et aqua peniteat.

V. 5.20 (f. 257ra) (= C. 5.[16].2, p. 274)

74. DE PUELLIS DISPONSATIS ET AB ALIIS RAPTIS. CONCILIO ANCIRANO.

Si puella disponsata et ab alio rapta fuerit ... similiter rapta si quandoque consenserit raptori.

V. 5.21 (f. 257ra) (= C. 5.[16].3, p. 275)

75. DE EO QUI CUM DISPONSATA ALTERIUS FORNICAVERIT. GREGORIUS.

Si quis cum disponsata alterius |p. 40| fornicatus ... a sacerdotii gradum non presumant umquam accedere.

V. 5.25 (f. 257va) (= C. 5.18.1, p. 275)

76. DE CONCUBINA. EX CONCILIO TOLLETANO.

De eo qui uxorem habet si concubinam habuerit ... |p. 41| ... donec desinat et ad penitentiam revertatur.

V. 5.34 (f. 259va)(= C. 5.26.2, pp. 277 f.)

77. DE EO QUI CONCUBINAM ANTEQUAM UXOREM HABET. IUDICIUM COMEANI.

Si quis laicus concubinam habens antequam uxorem accipiat, dimit(tat) eam .... et iii. annis peniteat quatenus circa qualitatem vel quantitatem culpae.

V. 5.35 (f. 259vb) (= C. 5.27.1, p. 278)

78. DE EO QUI UXOREM SIMUL ET CONCUBINAM |p. 42| HABET. CONCILIO TOLETANO.

Si quis habens uxorem simul et concubinam ... qualitatem sive quantitatem malignitatis suae perseverantia(m).

V. 5.38 (f. 260rb) (= C. 5.28.1, p. 278)

79. DE MULIERIBUS QUE LENOCINIUM FECERINT. CONCILI HELIBER(ITANO).

Mater vel pater vel qualibet fidelis si lenocinium ... suum placuit eam nec in finem accipere communionem.

V. 5.41 (f. 260va) (= C. 5.29.1, p. 279)

80. LAICUS PELLENS CONIUGEM SUAM COMMUNIONE PRIVETUR. IN CANONIBUS APOSTOLORUM.

Si quis laicus uxorem propriam pellens alteram vel ab alio dimissam duxerit communione privetur.

PRIVANDUM T V. 5.59 (f. 262vb) (= C. 5.34.3, p. 281)

81. DE EO QUI CUM ELECTA VIDUA FORNICAVERIT. |p. 43| SYNODUS ROMANA.

Si quis cum tali vidua qualem beatus apostolus Paulus... sed a sacerdotii gradus non presumant accedere.

V. 5.135 (f. 288ra) (= C. 5.67, pp. 304 f.)

82. DE EO QUI ACCEPERIT UXOREM EIUS QUI IN CAPTIVITATEM DUCTUS EST. IUDICIO PAPE LEONIS.

Si quis acceperit uxorem eius qui captivatus est ... |p. 44| ... acceperit in captivitate ducta est eo quod inscii fecerint.

V. 5.136 (f. 288ra) (= C. 5.68, p. 305)

83. DE ADULTERIO. DE HIS QUI ADULTERAS HABENT UXORES VEL SI IPSI ADULTERI COMPROBANTUR. CONCILIO ANCARANO.

Si cuius uxor adultera fuerit vel si ipse ... eum perfectionem consequi secundum pristinum gradum.

Titulus DE ADULTERIO V. 5.142 Titulus reliquus V. 5.143 (f. 289ra) (= C. 5.72.1 Titulus, C. 5.72.2 Textus, p. 306)

84. UT CUM FAMOSIS MALIS NON COMMUNICANDUM. GELASIUS PAPA.

Quos scimus sine ulla dubitatione esse fornicatores ... |p. 45| ... quos tali correctione corrigi non posse sentiunt.

V. 5.145 (f. 289rb) (= C. 5.72.7, p. 306)

85. DE EXCOMMUNICATIONE ADULTERI. SYNODUS ROMANA.

Omnes adulteri sive a celebratione misse sive a communione mense ... |p. 46| ... sive a comitatu usque dum penitentiam aga(n)t, excludendi sunt.

adulteros T V. 5.146 (f. 289va) (= C. 5.73.1, p. 306)

86. IOHANNES CONSTANTINOPOLITANUS EPISCOPUS ATQUE ALII ERUDITISSIMI VIRI PRUDENTES CONCILIORUM CANONUM DECRETALIUMQUE PONTIFICUM DE CONIUGIBUS ADULTER(IN)IS IUDICIU(M) EDIDERUNT. IMPRIMIS DE CONIUGATIS FORNICARIIS.

Si quis habens uxorem forsitan si cum muliere, et ipsae tamen vacans, ... |p. 47| virum par forma pudicitiae et continentiae inter virum et uxorem.

si cum] sicut T; vacanus T V. 5.149 (f. 289va) (= C. 5.74.1, p. 306)

87. DE LAICO QUI NON HABENS UXOREM SI PROXIMI SUI UXOREM MACULAVERIT. IUDICIO COMEANI.

Si quis laicus non habens uxorem si maculaverit uxorem proximi sui ... |p. 48| ... detestabilem providentia sacerdotis intuendum ita iudicaetur.

V. 5.150 (f. 289vb) (= C. 5.74.2, pp. 306 f.)

88. DE CONIUGIBUS. SI ADULTERATI HI INVENTI SUNT. IOHANNES CONSTANTINOPOLITANUS EPISCOPUS. SIMILITER THEODORUS ET COMEANUS.

Si quis uxorem suam invenerit adulteratam ... |p. 49| si invenerit adulterum non ad imperia iudicatur.

CONSTANTINOPOLITANUSQUE T   V. 5.151 (f. 290ra) (= C. 5.75, p. 307)

89. DE RECONCILIATIONE CONIUGIUM POST PURGATA ADULTERIA. AGATENSE.

Non aerit turpis neque difficilis etiam post perpetrata atque purgata ... non alias fiant quam conubia quae (con)vincuntur esse adulteria.

quam] quasi T   vincuntur T   V. 5.152 (f. 290ra) (= C. 5.76.1, p. 307)

90. IOHANNES CONSTANTINOPLITANUS EPISCOPUS.

Vir si voluntariae preter causa(m) fornicationis uxorem dimiserit suam nec tamen duxerit aliam, unde si illa forte ex hac occasione ... |pp. 50–53| ... viris ex hac causa sicut muliaeribus.

hoccasione T   V. 5.155.2 (f. 290vb) (= C. 5.78.3, p. 308) Quia paginae 50 et 51 ordinem foliorum non sequuntur, propterea canon continuatur in pagina 53.

91. DE HIS QUI CONSENTIUNT CONIUGIBUS SUIS FORNICARI. IOHANNES CONSTANTINOPLITANUS.

Si quis quod inlecebrosissimum turpeve (est) uxorem suam ab alio ... omnibus diebus vitae suae arbitrio periti sacerdotis cum flaetu et luctu penitere.

CONSTANTINOPLITANO T   V. 5.156 (f. 291ra) (= C. 5.79.1, p. 308)

92. DE HIS QUI CONIUGIBUS SUIS SE DIVIDUNT ET ALTERIS NUBUNT. IOHANNES CONSTANTINOPOLITANUS.

In multorum conciliis decretisque pontificum comperimus scriptum: Si quis quod deterius est suam uxorem preter fornicationem reliquerit ... |pp. 54–55| ... si vel e xii. annis vel minus circa compunctionem simul et emenda|p. 56|tionem ita arbitraetur.

CONSTANTINOPLITANO T conpugntionem T V. 5.158 (f. 291rb) (= C. 5.79.3, pp. 308 f.)

93. DE HIS QUI CONIUGATI SUNT SI DIMISSAS DUCUNT. IOHANNES CONSTANTINOPOLITANUS.

Si quis quod est mercatum incestuosum preter fornicationem uxorem suam ... |p. 57| ... iusta qualitatem et quantitatem criminis et conversationem simul et aemendationem.

DUCUNT] DICTAM T V. 5.160 (f. 291vb) (= C. 5.81, p. 309)

94. DE NON FORNICANTIBUS DIMISSIS. EXPOSITUM UT SUPRA.

Si que mulier non fornicans dimissa a viro et post illam aliam duxerit ... |p. 58| ... alii nupserit forsitan et vivente uxorae sua aliam ducit non habentem virum.

Titulus V. 5.162.1; Textus V. 5.162.2 (f. 292rb) (= C. 5.82.2 Titulus; C. 5.82.3 Textus, pp. 309 f.)

95. INSTITUTA PATRUM REGULA.

Si quis legitimam uxorem dimiserit et acceperit aliam ... communicet sed excommunicati a Christianis fiant.

V. 5.167.2 (f. 293vb) (= C. 5.84.2, p. 311)

96. DE CONSEN|p.59|SU CONIUGATIS IN SERVITIO DEI ACCEDERE.

Potest unus de coniugibus alteri dare licentiam ... |pp. 60–63| ... in viros et in feminas conservetur.

V. 5.170 (f.294va) (C. non invenitur)

97. AUGUSTINUS. SI MULIER MENSTRUA SIVE CONSUETE SI(VE)-INCONSUETE DEBET IN ECCLESIA(M)INTRARE AUT CORPUS DOMINI PERCIPERE. GREGORIUS.

|p. 64| Que tamen mulier dum consuaetudinem menstruam patitur ... superfluitas in culpa(m) non debet computari.

V. 5.180 (f. 297va) (= C. 5.92.2, p. 313)

98. IUDICIO THEODORI.

Animalia coitu hominis polluta occidantur carnesque ... in usu et coria ubi autem est dubium non occidantur.

coitum T V. 5.196.2 (f. 300ra) (= C. 5.98.2, p. 316)

99. DE MULIERE LIBERA SI SERVO SE COPULAVERIT. IUDICIUM COMEANI.

Mulier libera si servo marito se copulaverit et (ab) ambabus partibus nesciens esse servum ... |pp. 51–52| ... Quam sententiam tam libera cum servo quam liber cum ancilla patiatur.

libera interl. corr. vidua T ambobus T V. 5.206 (f. 302rb) (= C. 5.101.6–7, pp. 318 f.)

100. DE PROPINQUITATE CONSANGUINIS SUI MORE PECORUM COMMIXTI. IDEM PRO ABSIT PRIMA VEL SECUNDA. IUDICIUM CUMMEANI.

Si quis more pecorum cum propinqua sanguinis sui incestis ... |p. 65| ... ad extremum vitae tantum communione mereantur.

PROPINQUITATES T pecorum] peccatorum T sui] sive T communione mereantur] commaereantur T V. 5.222 (f. 309rb) (= C. 5.109.3, p. 328)

101. DE SEPARATIONE INLICITIS CONIUGIBUS ET DE IUDICIIS EORUM. CONCILIO NICENO.

Si quis duxerit de propria cognatione in coniugium ... |p. 66| ... sive amplius iuxta prolixiores perpetrationes peccati.

ET IUDICES T; 3 in coniugio T V. 5.226 (f. 309vb) (= C. 5.110.2, p. 329)

102. DE VIRO AUT MULIERE SI AD DOMINUM POST PECCATUM SUUM FUERINT CONVERSI A(B)INVICEM SEPARENTUR. SINODUS HIBERNENSI(S).

Vir autem sive mulier cum ad Dominum conversi fuerint post peccatum suum ... |p. 67| ... de re inlicita quiaescat, sed cum affuerit cito veniam a Deo paetant.

V. 5.229 (f. 310rb) (= C. 5.111, p. 329)

103. DE MULIERE QUE DUOBUS FRATRIBUS NUPSERIT. IUDICIUM COMMEANI.

Mulier si duobus fratribus nupserit abici eam ... |p. 68| ... tam mulieres quam viri tenere debent.

V. 5.230 (f. 310va) (= C. 5.112, p. 329)

104. DE INCESTIS CONIUN(C)TIONIBUS VEL DIVERSIS COMMIXTIONIBUS. CONCILIO AGATENSE. SIMILITER PAPA GREGORIUS DECREVIT.

Incesti dicuntur propter illicitam commixtionem. Vocati ... |pp. 69–72| ... vel quantitatem seu etiam intentione fornicationis.

V. 5.231 (f. 310va. Textus Vaticanus terminat "... aut uxor fratris aut socrum" f.310vb in calce in medio canonis.) (= C. 5.113, pp. 329 f.)

105. DE HOMINIBUS QUI SUOS FILIOS NESCIENTE(S) SUSCEPISSENT. EPISTULA GURDIANI EPISCOPI.

Deusdedit sanctae et apostolicae Romanae aecclesiae episcopus Gurdiano Hispaniaensis ecclesiae coepiscopo et fratri dilecto. Pervenit ad nos diaconus vester vestrae sanctitatis aepistolam ferens quod quidam viri et mulieres ... |pp. 73–74| ... Decrevit sancta synodus: Si pater aut mater proprium filium a sacro baptismate suscaeperit, hi omnino a coniugio separentur.

V. Index 5.234 (f. 253rb) (= C. 5.114.2, pp. 332 f.)

106. NON LICEAT FILIAM SUAM QUIS DE SACRO FONTE FILIO SUO NATURALI IN MATRIMONIUM TRADERE. PAPAE ZA|p. 75|CHARIE. SIMILITER DEUSDEDIT SU(M)MUS SACERDOS.

Quoniam non oportet filiam de sacro quam fonte susceperit ... conscii simul cum auctore sit ista conditio.

MATRIMONIO T   V. Index 5.237 (f. 253rb) (= C. 5.117.2, p. 334)

107. Quod non oportet a septuagesima usque in oc|p. 76|tavas paschae ... nuptias celebrare, quod si factum fuerit separentur.

Burch. 9.4 (PL 140: 816)

108. UT NULLUM CONIUGIUM SINE DOTE FIAT. EX CONCILIO ARELATENSE.

Nullum coniugium sine dote fiat iusta possibilitatem ... sine publicis nuptiis quisquam nubaere presumat

Burch. 9.6 (PL 140.816)

109. DE PRIMO CONIUGIO. EX CONCILIO MEDIOLANO.

In primo coniugio debent presbiteri missam agere et benedicere ambos et postea abstineant ab aecclesia xxx. diebus.

Burch. 9.8 (PL 140: 816)

110. DE VIRGINIBUS QUE VIRGINITATEM ANTE NUPTIAS NON CUSTODIERINT. |p. 77| EX CONCILIO ELIBERTANO.

Virgines que virginitatem non custodiaerint si eosdem qui ... quinquennium peniteant, et sic ad communionem accedant.

QUAE] QUI T   Burch. 9.14 (PL 140: 817)

111. DE INGENUO HOMINE SI ALTERIUS ANCILLAM PRO INGENUA ACCEPERIT ET POST ANCILLA(M) EAM (ESSE) INTELLEXERIT. EX CONCILIO APUD VERMERIAM CIVITATEM (CUI INTER)FUIT PIPINUS REX.

Si quis ingenuus homo alterius ancillam ... |p. 78| ... mulier ingenua de servo debet facere.

INGENIO T   Burch. 9.26 (PL 140: 819)

112. DE FEMINA INGENUA SI MARITUM SERVUM ACCEPERIT. EX EODEM CONCILIO.

Si femina ingenua acceperit servum sciens quia servus ... una lex aerit et viro et faeminae.

Burch. 9.27 (PL 140: 819)

113. EX CONCILIO AGATENSI.

Dictum est enim nobis quod quidam legitima servorum matrimonia ... |p. 79| ... ubi legalis coniunctio fuit et per voluntatem dominorum.

Burch. 9.29 (PL 140: 819)

114. Fecisti homicidium voluntariae sine necessitate non in hostae ... |pp. 79–82| ... ingrediatur monasterium monachorum et ibi iugiter Deo serviat.

Burch. 19.5 (PL 140: 951 f.)

115. DE UTRIUSQUE CONIUGII COMPATRIBUS. EX CONCILIO ARELATENSE.

Si unus ex coniugibus filium aut filia(m) alterius de sacro fonte suscep(er)it ... parentibus infantis quia vir et mulier caro una effecti sunt.

COMPATRES T V. Index 5.238 (f.253rb) (= C. 5.118, p. 334)

116. DE HIS QUI CUM FILIA SPIRITUALI FORNICAVERINT. IUDICIUM COMEANI.

Si quis cum filia spirituali fornicaverit |p. 83| et ipsa tamen simplice muliaere ... |pp. 83–84| ...presbitero vel diacono tale scelus commiserit.

F. 2.79.2 (= C. 2.35.2, p. 86)

117. DE HIS QUI ADULTERA(N)T OPUS DEI ID EST FORMAM CREATURAM CREATORIS MAXIME MULIERES QUE SE DECORANT CANDORE COLORE PLACERE HOMINIBUS.

Sanctus Ambrosius in tractatu Exameron opus Dei ab homine immutari terribiliter prohibet dicens: Mulier habens artificem atque pictorem Dominum ... |pp. 85–86| ... quod decolorare se colore candoris pro hominibus placere presumunt.

MAXIMA T V. Index 5.239 (f. 253rb) (= C. 5.120, pp. 334 f.)

118. Synodus Romana.

Si que creatoris deformat creaturam ac Dei opus |p. 87| adulteraverit iii. annis peniteat.

C. 5.120, pp. 335 f.

119. Interdixit per omnia sancta synodus non episcopo ... que a masculo subveniri non possit.

F. 2.16 (= C. 2.9.1, p. 72)

120. DE SUSPECTA SACERDOTUM INFAMATIONE.

Eugenius episcopus. Si quispiam sacerdotum id est aepiscopus ... |p. 88| ... maxime ab omni femina sit abstinendus.

F. 2.32 (= C. 2.25.1, p. 80)

121. CUIUSCUMQUE ORDINIS CLERICI NUPTIALIA CONVIVIA VITENT NE SACER AUDITUS AUT OPTUTUS POLLUI POSSIT. CONCILIO AGATENSE.

Presbiteri, diacones, subdiacones vel quibus ducendi uxores licentia non est ... |p. 89| ... turpium spectaculorum atque verborum contagio polluantur.

F. 2.49 (= C. 2.21, p. 79)

122. DE CLERICI(S) QUI POST CONVERSIONEM VEL HONOREM CUM UXORIBUS FORNICAVERINT. DECRETALIUM PATRUM CLERICORUM.

Si quis aepiscopus, presbiter, diaconus etiam monachus qui uxorem habuit ... |p. 90| ... ob(e)dire noluaerint aecclesiae communione priventur.

F. 2.58 (= C. 2.28, p. 83)

123. DE CONCUPISCENTIA NON CONSUMATA.

In canone Neocesariensis ita habeatur: Placuit ut si quis concupiscens mulierem ... |p. 91| ... insp(ic)iendum in qua fornicatus est ita paeniteat.

F. 2.67 (= C. 2.36.1, p. 86)

124. IUDICIUM THEODORI.

Si quis diu cum muliere aut puella nititur fornicari ... in pane et aqua, clericus et laicus duo(bus) anni(s) peniteat.

F. 2.67.2 (= C. 2.36.2, p. 86)

125. Qui concupiscit mente fornicari et non potuerit aut mulier vel puella non susceperit eum ... non est susceptus ab aea xl. dies peniteat.

F. 2.67.2 (= C. 2.36.2, p. 86)

126. DE EPISCOPO, PRESBITERO |p. 92| VEL DIACONO QUI UXOREM DUXERIT. EX EPISTULA SIRICI(I) PAPAE AD GENESIUM EPISCOPUM.

Qui ordinatus est aepiscopus vel presbiter aut diaconus et in aliquo tempore missam fecit et postea uxorem duxerit ... . sit in potestate aepiscopi quid de ea facere velit.

F. 2.69 (= C. 2.38.1, p. 87)

127. DE CLERICO QUI POST LEVITICA(M) BENEDICTIONEM |p. 93| PRESUMPSERIT UXOREM DUCERE AUT FORNICATUS FUERIT. CONCILIO NEOCESARIENSE.

Presbiter si post leviticam benedictionem uxorem ... abiciet ad penitentiam inter laicos redigi oportet.

F. 2.70 (= C. 2.38.2, p. 87)

128. DE CLERICO QUI POST LEVITICAM BENEDICTIONEM VEL CONCUBINAS AUT QUASI UXORES HABERE PRESUMPSERIT. SINODUS ROMANA.

De illis videlicet sacerdotibus qui per ignominiam ... |pp. 94–95| ... perseveraverit usque in finem hic salvus aerit.

F. 2.73 (= C. 2.39.1, pp. 87 f.)

129. IUDICIUM DE FEMINA QUE IN FORNICATIONE REPREHENSA EST CUM EPISCOPO AUT PRESBITERO VEL DIACONO AUT QUASI CONIUGIO COPULATA. EX EPISTULA HORMISDE PAPE SIMILITER EUGENII PAPE, THEODORUS EPISCOPUS ET COMEANUS ARCHIMANDRITA QUASI UNO ORE CONSTITUERUNT.

Si qua femina in fornicatione deprehensa fuerit ... |pp. 96–100| ... turpissimam inlecebrissimamque catena tenetur constricta potuissent.

UMO HORE T F. 2.75 (= C. 2.40, pp. 88 f.)

130. DE HIS QUI INFRA ECCLESIAM INFOR(NICA)VERINT VEL ADULTERAVERINT. IUDICIUM SINODALE.

In presentiarum nichil periculosius quam peccare letaliter ... |pp. 101–102| ... turpiter consentiens sic tamen ut decet mulieres.

F. 2.78.1 (= C. 2.34.1, pp. 83 f.)

131. SEQUITUR.

Si quis autem sacerdos cum filia sua |p.103| spirituali fornicaverit ... et cunctis diebus vitae suae ibi serviat Domino.

F. 2.79.1 (= C. 2.35.1, p. 86)

132. DE HIS QUI CUM FILIA SPIRITUALI FORNICAVERI(N)T. IUDICIO COMEANI.

Si quis cum filia spirituali et ipsa tamen simplex mulier ... |pp. 104–105| ... presbitero vel diacono tale scelus vel vitium commiserit.

Titulus F. 2.79.1 textus F. 2.79.2 (= C. 2.35.2, p. 86)

133. QUI CUM UXORE PRO DEO RELICTA FORNICAVERIT. IUDICIO COMEANI.

Si quis cum ea quam propter Deum reliquit uxore fornicaverit ... laicus v., ii. ex his in pane et aqua.

Deum quis reliquit uxorem T F. 2.77 (= C. 2.41.2, p. 89)

134. DE CLERICIS. SI PRO CRIMINALIBUS CULPIS DAMPNATI FUERINT MINIME COMMUNIONE PRIVENTUR. IN CANONIBUS APOSTOLORUM.

Episcopus aut presbiter seu diaconus qui in homicidium aut in adulterium vel fornicationem ... |p. 106| ... Dominus bis inidipsum, similiter reliqui ministri aecclesiae.

F. 2.82.1 (= C. 2.43.1, p. 89)

135. DE ADULTERIIS HONERATORUM CLERICORUM. IUDICIUM CANONUM.

De adulteris honeratorum id observandum est ... sunt crimina, communione concessa, ab ordine degradetur.

F. 2.84 (= C. 2.45.1, p. 90)

136. QUOD CLERICI NON DEPONENDI SUNT AB UNO EPISCOPO. EX CONCILIO EXSPALENSE.

|p. 107| De presbiteris et diaconibus ab uno episcopo non deponendis ... qui indiscusco potestate tyrannica non auctoritate canonica dampnant.

auctoritate tyrannica T F. 2.90.1 (= C. 2.50, p. 91)

137. SEQUITUR.

Episcopus enim sacerdotibus ac ministris solus honorem dare potest ... quod canones de illis precipiunt diffinire.

F. 2.90.2 (= C. 2.50, p. 91)

138. DE EO QUI POSTQUAM SE DEO VOVE|p. 108|RIT AD SECULARE(M) HABITUM REVERTITUR ET DE STULTIS VOTIS. IUDICIUM COMEANI.

Si quis clericus aut monachus postquam se Deo voverit ... si tale scelus ammiserit pari sententia subiaceat.

F. 2.134 (= C. 2.79.2, p. 106)

139. SEQUITUR.

Si quis vir vel si quae mulier votum habens virginitatis ... |p. 109| ... sic stulta vota frangenda sunt et importabilia.

F. 2.134 (= C. 2.79.2, p. 106)

140. DE HIS QUI POST SANCTE RELIGIONIS PROFESSIONEM SECULAREM HABITUM SUMUNT. EX CONCILIO ARELATENSE.

Hi qui post sanctae religionis professionem apostantur ... si presumpserit ab aecclesia alienus efficitur.

F. 2.135 (= C. 2.79.3, p. 106)

141. DE VIRGINIBUS VELATIS SI |p. 110| DEVIAVERINT.

Item que Christo spiritualiter nubunt et a sacerdote velantur ... et postea ad humanas nuptias transmigravit.

F. 2.137 (= C. 2.81, p. 106)

142. SI SPONSALIUM INTER SPONSUM ET SPONSAM FACTA FUERINT ET UNUS EX HIS IN MONASTERIO INTRAVERI(T). IUSTINIANUS REX.

Si sponsalia legitime inter sponsum et sponsam ... |p. 111| ... reddatur et pena utrique parte remittatur.

F. 2.159 (= C. 2.94, p. 109)

143. DE MONACHO QUI UXOREM ACCIPIT VEL MONACHA MARITUM. SIRICIUS PAPA.

Monachus si uxorem accipit in fine communicet; similiter et monacha si maritum accipit.

F. 2.170 (= C. 2.101.2, p. 113)

144. DE PENITENTIA MONACHORUM QUI FILIOS GENUERINT. SYNODUS ROMANA.

Monachi qui procreantes filios in carcere retrudantur ... solius |p. 112| misericordiae intuitu communioni possit gratia indulgeri.

gratiam T F. 2.171 (C. 2.101.3, p. 113)

145. UT SACRARIUM MULIERES NON INTROEANT. EX CONCILIO LAODOCENSE.

Quod non oporteat mulieres ingredi ad altare.

F. 2.174.1 (= C. 2.104.1, p. 113)

146. Item. In decretalibus Pape Gelasii

Nichilominus inpatienter audivimus tantum divinarum rerum ... que non nisi virorum famulatui deputanda sunt sexus.

F. 2.174.2 (= C. 2.104.2, p. 113)

147. DE ABBATE QUI REM MOBILEM DE SUA ECCLESIA DISTRAXERIT. SYNODUS ROMANA.

Si quis abbas rem mobilem sive inmobilem distraxerit ... |p. 113| ... et quamdiu tenuerit communione privatus sit.

F. 2.186 (= C. 2.111, p. 115)

148. UT MULIERES IN MONASTERIO VIRORUM INGREDI NON DEBEAN(T) NEC EAS MONACHI COMATRE(S)PRESUMANT. Gregorius Valentiano abbati.

Pervenit ad nos quod in monasterium tuum passim mulieres ascendant ... |p. 114| ... emendationis tue qualitate ceteri sine dubio corrigantur.

MONACHA T F. 2.195 (= C. 2.118, p. 117)

149. EX DECRETO PAPE GELASII.

Baptizandi sibi quispiam passim quocumque tempore ... salutari for|p. 115|tassis egrotans et exitio preventus abscedat.

F. 3.11.2 (= C. 3.2.3, p. 123)

150. DE SACERDOTE QUI BAPTISMUM DENEGAVERIT. GREGORIUS.

Si quis sacerdos baptismum cuiquam in periculo positus ... et luctu inter laicos paenitentiae se subdat.

F. 3.35 (= C. 3.28.3, p. 128)

151. DE HIS QUI BAPTISMUM ITERANT. SINODUS NICENA.

Qui rebaptizatus fuerit ignorans non indiget ... |p. 116| ... non recte baptizante, iterum debet baptizari.

F. 3.44 (= C. 3.30, pp. 128 f.)

152. DE HIS QUI SINE BAPTISMO MORIUNTUR. IUDICIUM THEODORI.

Cuius parvulus per neglegentiam sine baptismo moritur ... |p. 117| ... eum fraudavit unde aeterna requie exclusus est.

F. 3.46.1 (= C. 3.28.1, p. 128)

153. DE BAPTIZATO ET NON CHRISMATO AB EPISCOPO MORITUR. IUDICIUM THEODORI.

Si cuius parvulus per neglegentiam sine chrismate ab episcopo ... iii. annos peniteat, si vero sine neglegentia.

F. 3.47.1 (= C. 3.28.4, p. 128)

154. Item in concilio Aurasico. De eo autem qui baptismate quacumque necessitate faciente non chrismatus fuerit in confirmatione sacerdotis commonebitur.

F. 3.47.2 (= C. 3.28.5, p. 128)

155. DE DIE DOMINICO. HIERONYMUS.

Die sancto dominico nulli opus terrenum agere licebit ... |p. 118| ... per inobedientiam evacuare contendit anathe|p. 119|mate percellatur.

Titulus F. 3.53.1 textus F. 3.53.2 (= C. titulus 3.33.3; textus 3.33.4, p. 130)

156. DE DISTRICTIONE QUI DECIMAS DARE NOLUIT. LUDOVICUS REX.

De his qui decimas iam per multos annos aut ex parte ... unde hanc decimam persolui debuit amissurum se sciat.

F. 3.66 (= C. 3.44.1, p. 133)

157. UT DECIMAS IN QUATTUOR PARTES DIVIDANT. REGULA CANONICA.

|p. 120| Sacerdotes ut levitae populo suscipiant decimas ... ad dispensandum erga omnes qui indigent cum timore Dei.

F. 3.74 (= C. 3.48.2, p. 135)

158. DE HIS (QUI RES) PAUPERUM IN USUM PROPRIUM VERTUNT. HIERONYMUS.

Simplicit(er) intellectus hedificat auditorem dum tante Dominus ... |p. 121| ... nephas nobis quam eidem tribuit exemplum.

F. 3.101 (= C. 3.67.1, p. 139)

159. DE OBLATIONIBUS ECCLESIE QUE MINISTRIS ECCLESIE CONFERUNTUR. CONCILIO CANGRENSE.

Si quis oblationes aecclesiae ad aecclesiam accipere vel dare ... nec cum eis voluerit agere consilio anathema sit.

F. 3.106 (= C. 3.71.2, p. 140)

160. DE HIS QUI ECCLESIASTICA MISTERIA PRETER ECCLESIA(M) FACIUNT. EX CONCILIO GANGNENSI.

Si quis extra aecclesia(m) seorsum con |p. 122| conventus celebrat ... conveniente presbitero iusta decretum episcopi anathema sit.

F. 3.107 (= C. 3.72.1, p. 140)

161. DE HIS QUI SUAS VEL PROPINQUORUM OBLATIONES ECCLESIA FRAUDANT. AGATENSE.

Clerici etiam vel seculares qui oblationes parentum ... velud necatores pauperum quousque reddantur anathematizentur.

F. 3.114 (= C. 3.74.3, pp. 140 f.)

162. DE CLERICI(S) ARTIFICIOSIS SI COLLECTA PECUNIA NON PLUS EXIGANT QUAM NECESSITA(S) EXIGIT.

|p. 123| Paterius. Si quis clericus acceperit permissionem pontificis ... non tradat aliis nam si tradiderit peccatum facit.

F. 3.120 (= C. 3.77.1, p. 141)

163. UT NULLUS FACULTATES USURPET ECCLESIAE. Synodus Romana.

Qui facultatem ecclesiasticam subsidio vite congregant ... a Christiani fiant, |p. 124| donec penitentiam trium annorum agant.

F. 3.145 (= C. 3.[92], pp. 144 f.)

164. DE MANENDO IN LOCO PROPRIO ET FACIENDO VOLUNTATEM DEI IN EO.

Augustinus. In toto orbem terrarum instituta sunt regna celorum ... fidem habes in Domino et permane in loco tuo.

F. 3.173 (= C. 3.111.1, p. 148)

165. DE MUTATIONE LOCI PRO SALUTE ANIME.

Valet interdum conversis pro salutae anime ... quisque vixit in aspectu mentis opponitur.

F. 3.174 (= C. 3.111.2, pp. 148 f.)

166. CLERICI NEC |p. 125| VESTIMENTIS NEC CALCIAMENTIS QUERA(N)T DECOREM. CONCILIO AGATHENSE.

Clericus professionem suam etiam abitu et incessu ... nec vestibus nec calciamentis decorem quaerat.

F. 3.197 (= C. 3.128.2, p. 154)

167. DE CLERICIS DIMISSIS. SYNODUS ROMANA.

Si quis a se vel parentibus suis voluntarie ... sub trecentorum x. et viii. patrum |p. 126| anathemate maledictionis maneat.

F. 3.210 (= C. 3.133, p. 155)

168. DE SACRAMENTIS ECCLESIE. Clemens Iacobo karissimo.

Tribus gradibus divinorum secretorum commissa sint ... |pp. 127–130| ... qui digne possint dominica sacramenta tractare.

F. 3.218 (= C. 3.141.1, pp. 157 f.)

169. DE PALLIS ET VELIS ALTARIS.

Pallas vero et vela ea quae in sacrario ... |pp. 131–132| ... Dominum loquentem per te ipse sibi dampnationem accipiat.

PALAS T F. 3.228.1 (= C. 3.147.1, p. 160)

170. CONSTITUTA BONIFATII.

Ut nulla mulier vel monacha pallam sacratam ... vel lavare aut in ecclesia ponere incensum.

F. 3.228.2 (= C. 3.147.2, pp. 160 f.)

171. Clemens Iacobo karissimo.

De vasis sacris ita gerendum |p. 133| est ... non iaceant ne de introitu pedum inquinentur.

F. 3.229 (= C. 3.148.1, p. 161)

172. QUOD MINISTRI ALTARIS OBLATIONE CELEBRATA DEBEANT COMMUNICARE. IN CANONIBUS APOSTOLORUM.

Si quis episcopus aut presbiter aut diaconus vel quilibet ex sacerdotali cathalogo ... |p. 134| ... de eo qui sacrificavit quod recte non obtulerit.

CELEBRARE T qualibet T F. 3.236 (= C. 3.151, pp. 161 f.)

173. DE TACITURNITATE IN ECCLESIA. CANONICA REGULA.

Omni tempore in ecclesia tam a popolo quam a clero ... fecerit corporali disciplinae |p. 135| subitiatur ut ceteri timeant.

F. 3.240 (= C. 3.154.1, p. 162)

174. Ut clerici edendi vel bibendi causa tabernas non ingrediantur nisi peregrinationis necessitate compulsi.

F. 3.243.2 (= C. 3.156.2, p. 162)

175. ITEM.

Clericus qui non pro emendo aliquid ... in foro deambulatat ab officio suo degradetur.

premendo T F. 3.244.2 (= C. 3.157.1, p. 162)

176. CONCILIO CARTHAGINIENSE.

Clericos scurrilles et verbis turpibus insistentes ab officio suo negradandos.

F. 3.246.1 (= C. 3.158.1, pp. 162 f.)

177. Item.

Clerici inter aepulas cantantes supra dicte sententiae severitate feriantur.

F. 3.246.2 (= C. 3.148.1, p. 163)

178. Clerici in quacumque seditione arma volumptariae sumpserint ammisso ordinis sui gradu, in monasterio retrudantur penitentiae.

F. 3.249.1 (= C. 3.161.1, p. 163)

179. SINODUS ROMANA.

Si quis venationes quascumque |p. 136| exercuerit si clericus i. anno in pane et aqua peniteat, presbiter iii., diaconus ii.

F. 3.252.2 (= C. 3.162.5, p. 163)

180. ORDO DEFUNCTORUM. De his ita Augustinus in libro De Cura Gerenda pro Mortuis et in libro Civitatis Dei.

Qui[1] facit, inquit, exequias ob amore(m) illius facit qui promisit corpora resurrectura. Necque enim contempnenda sunt et abicienda corpora defunctorum, et maxime fidelium quibus tamquam organis et vasis ad omnia opera bona usus est Spiritus sanctus. Unde et antiquorum fidelium funera officio sapiaetate curata sunt et exequie celebrate ac sepulture provisae. Ipsique cumviverent de sepeliendis seu transferendis suis corporibus filiis mandaverunt |p. 137| et Tobias mortuos sepeliendo Deum promeruisse commendatur. Ipse Dominus die tertio resurrecturus religiose mulieres opus bonum predicit predicandum et Ioseph qui eum sepelivit mire collaudatur. Ac ideo sic pro nostris defunctis certare debemus quatenus possint participes fieri eorum quos[2] Christus revocavit a claustris inferni. Simili etiammodo celebramus officia pro ipsis quomodo celebratur in illis diebus quando Christus descendit ad inferna in quibus et creditur mortuus. Denique in aliquibus locis generaliter pro omnibus defunctis omni tempore excepto Pentecostes et festis diebus oratur in officio vespertinali; in aliquibus pro eis |p. 138| missa celebratur; in kalendarum etiam diebus seu anniversariis per viiii. Psalmos et responsa et lectiones, similimodo officia persolvuntur. Et ideo iusta

Augustinum: Non sunt pretermittende supplicationes pro spiritibus mortuorum quae sunt faciende[3] pro omnibus Christianis fidelibus etiam tacitis nominibus. Quorum sub generali commemoratione suscipit ecclesia[4], ut quibus ista desunt parentes aut filii aut qualescumque cognati vel amici, ab una ei(s)exibeatur matre communi. Si autem deessent iste supplicationes quae fiunt recta et pia fide pro mortuis, puto quod nichil prodesse spiritibus eorum si qui(bus)libet locis sanctis proponenda essent exanimata[5] |p. 139| corpora. Quapropter rite caelebrantur illi tres dies generaliter ab omnibus infra xxx. qui voca(n)tur tertius, vii^{mus} xxx^{mus}. De tertio enim die et septimo ita habetur in libro Numerorum (19.11): Qui tetigerit cadaver hominis et propter (hoc) fuerit inmundus vii diebus aspargatur aqua lustrationibus die iii. (et) vii. et sic mundabitur. Inmunditia haec protractu cadaveris animam pollutam significat operibus mortuis et quia neglexit cultum Dei. In cogitatione in vita et intellectu humiliter confitendo offerimus sacrificium Deo (die) iii.; commendati defuncti possumus ad memoriam reducere tertiam diem resurrectionis Domini in qua devoti|p.140|us est generaliter supplicandum. De vii. vero die habemus auctoritatem in libro Genesaeos (50.10). Mortuo enim Iacob in Egipto et translato a Ioseph trans Iordanen cum comitatu maximo celebraverunt exsequias cum planctu magno et fecerunt septem dies. Et alibi luctus mortui vii. dies facti[6] autem omnes dies vitae eius. Quod autem apud aliquos viiii. dies celebratur et vocabatur Novehdial id est Nonagenarius. Augustinus. In libro Quaestionum redarguit maxime cum nullus sanctorum hoc fecisse probatur cum sit consuetudo gentilium. Sane vii. dies auctoritatem in Scripturis habent quia septenarius |p. 141| numerus propter sabbati sacramentum precipuae indicium quiaetis est. Unde merito mortuis tamquam requiescentibus exhibetur. De xxx^{mo} die scriptum est in libro Numerorum (20.30): Omnis autem multitudo videns occubuisse Aaron flevit Israel (super) eo xxx. diebus. David et filii Israel ieiunaverunt pro Saul et planxerunt planctu[7] magno. Et in libro Sapientiae (Ecclesiasticus 38.16) de tertio et vii. et xxx. die. Fili in mortuum produc lacrimas et postpauca: Propter delaturam autem amare[8] fer luctum illius uno diae et iterum: Fac luctum (secundum) meritum eius uno die vel duobus propter detractionem. Ubi primo dixit propter delaturam uno die fer luctum, |p. 142| postea propter detractionem uno vel duobus diebus, tres dies introduxit in luctum. Quapropter et nos pro valde helemosinis ieiunare seu helemosinas facere atque interitus pro eorum aerratibus flere debaemus ut quod illi in vita debuerunt facere et non faecerunt saltim nos pro illis cum Dei auxilio impleamus. Interea ea dicunt aliquis: Si pro omnibus Christianis licitum sit missas celebrare. Hunc Agustinus. Necque negandum est defunctorum animas pietate suorum inventium revelari cum pro illis sacrificium mediatori offertur vel in ecclesia helemosinae fiunt set eis haec prosunt qui cum viverent hec sibi ut postea prodesse |p. 143| posse meruerunt. Est enim quidam vivendi modus nec tam bonus ut non requirat ista post mortem nec tam malus ut eis non prosint ista post mortem. Est vero talis in bono ut his haec non requirat et est rursus talis in malo ut nec his valeat cum ab hac vita transierit adiuvari. Quapropter oportet pro ovnibus regeneratis ista facere ut nullus eorum pretermittatur ad quos hec beneficia possint et debeant pervenire, presertim cum quidam ab ostibus captus vinculisque ferribus mancipatus[9] a quodam servo D(e)i scilicet germano suo ut putabatur mortuus celebratis cotidie |p. 144| pro eis missis more mortuorum sepissime vincula solverentur a quibus postea absolutus est. Sed haec notandum quia misse mortuorum absque Gloria et absque Alleluia seu pacis osculo celebrantur quae est indicium letitiae. Ad imitationem agitur officiorum que aguntur in morte Domini. Potest hoc addi in (h)omelia Origenis quinta libri Levitici ubi licit(um) sacrificium pro peccato non fit in oleo. Dicitur enim non superponi oleum letitiae nec thus suavitatis imponitur. Ac ideo absque Gloria et Alleluia celebratur quia sine oleo et thure Romani in vespertinis seu vigiliis atque matutinis defunctorum tres tantummodo |p. 145| Psalmos recitant, scilicet ob sepulturam Domini triduanam. At hi qui per nonarium numerum sicuti est in kalendarum dierum seu anniversariorum recolunt figurant illa officia nocturnalia que in passione Domini rite celebrantur. Anniversaria dies ideo repetitur pro defunctis quoniam nescimus qualiter eorum causa habeatur in alia vita. Quapropter imitandum nobis est assiduae summa largitate venerari imitationem sacre integritatis in orationibus fidelium defunctorum ut eis augeatur divina clementia.

In Collectione in V Libris non invenitur. Cf. PL 101: 1277–1280.

[1] qui quid T [2] quos] quod T [3] faciende] faciendas T [4] ecclesia] ecclesiam T [5] exanimata] examinata T [6] facti] fatui T [7] planctum T [8] amare] a matre T [9] mancipatis T

181. UT A IEIUNIS SACERDOTIBUS DEO SACRIFICIA CELEBRANTUR. CONCILIO AFRICANO.

Ut sacramenta altaris non nisi a ieiunis hominibus ... |p. 146| ... si illi qui faciunt iam pransi inveniantur.

alterius T ieiuniis T F. 3.257 (= C. 3.167, p. 164)

182. QUOD FIDELES LAICI INGREDIENTES ECCLESIAS COMMUNICARI DEBEANT. IN CANONIBUS APOSTOLORUM.

Omnes fideles qui ingrediuntur aecclesiam et scripturas ... inquietudines aecclesiae commoventes convenit communione privari.

F. 3.271.1 (= C. 3.177.1, p. 167)

183. UT SACRAMENTA DOMINI PASSI(M) NON DENTUR.

Clemens. Preci(pi)mus ne cui extero ab aecclesia ... |p. 147| ... ante triduum profitetur panes propositionis manducavit.

2 ne cui] nec cui T F. 3.273 (= C. 3.179, p.167)

184. NEC LAICI NEC FEMINE INGREDIANTUR AD ALTARE.

Synodus Bracarensis. Laici seu femine non ingrediantur ad altare ad communicandum. Si autem presumpserint, aecclesiasticae correptioni subiaceant.

F. 3.275 (= C. 3.181, p. 167)

185. |p. 148| Fecisti omicidium pro vindictia parentum, si fecisti xl. dies ... Dominus dicit michi vindicatam ego retribuam.

Burch. 19.5 (PL 140: 952)

186. Si fecisti omicidium nolens ita in ira ... de homicidiis sponte |p. 149|commissis constitutum est.

Burch. 19.5 (PL 140: 952)

187. Fecisti homicidium in bello iussu legitimi ... vel xl. dies cum vii. sequentibus annis.

Burch. 19.5 (PL 140: 952)

188. Occidisti tu liber servum senioris tui ... et senior tuus similiter nisi servus sit fur aut latro et pro pace aliorum fieri precipiat.

Burch. 19.5 (PL 140: 952)

189. |p. 150| Si autem tu servus conservum tuum iussu ... excepto sine pro pace communi fieret.

Burch. 19.5 (PL 140: 952)

190. Consiliatus es homicidium et non fecisti et occisus ... pane et aqua cum vii. sequentibus annis paeniteat.

Burch. 19.5 (PL 140: 952–953)

191. Explorasti vel speculatus (es) aliquem hominem ... sequentes annos ita observes |p. 151| ut consuetudo est.

Burch. 19.5 (PL 140: 953)

192. Fuistis cum aliis qui pugnaverunt contra aliquem ... vii. sequentibus annis ita observes ut consuetudo est.

Burch. 19.5 (PL 140: 953)

193. Fecisti patricidium id est interfecisti patrem ... |pp. 152–153| ... conversationem tuam aut extendere vel minuere valeat.

Burch. 19.5 (PL 140: 953)

194. Fecisti homicidium casu ita ut nullus occidere ... |pp. 154–157| ... quam illud quod industria factum est.

Burch. 19.5 (PL 140: 953–954)

195. Occidisti seniorem tuum vel in concilio fuisti ... eo fuerit impetrata simplici animo observa.

Burch. 19.5 (PL 140: 954)

196. |p. 158| Secundum aut concilium est tale arma depone ... |p. 159| ... si observaveris consilium ut accipias tibi concedimus.

Burch. 19.5 (PL 140: 954)

197. Occidisti aut in consilio fuisti ut occideretur ... |p. 160| ... de his qui homicidia sponte et per cupiditatem commiserunt.

Burch. 19.5 (PL 140: 954–955)

198. Fecisti truncatione(m) manuum aut pedum aut oculos ... unum annum per legitimas ferias penitere debes.

Burch. 19.5 (PL 140: 955)

199. Interfecisti furem aut latronem ubi comprehendi ... |p. 161| ... cum mediocri cervisa utere et temperare.

Burch. 19.5 (PL 140: 955)

200. Si autem sine odii meditatione te tuaque liberando ... |p. 162| ... non deponatur tamen quandiu vivat penitentiam agat.

Burch. 19.5 (PL 140: 955)

201. Accusasti aliquem et per tuam accusationem ... tres quadragesimas per legitimas ferias penitere debes.

Burch. 19.5 (PL 140: 955)

202. Cepisti aliquem et tradidisti eum in tale locum ... ratione eum illuc traderes ut vel debilitavetur vel occideretur.

Burch. 19.5 (PL 140: 955)

203. |p. 163| Occidisti tu ipse aut aliquis per tuum consilium ... |pp. 164–165| ... iii. dies per ebdomadas ut perfectus purificari merearis.

Burch. 19.5 (PL 140: 955–956)

204. Fecisti periurium per cupiditatem xl. dies in pane et aqua ... |p. 166| ... et monasterium ingressus iugitur penitentie se subdat.

Burch. 19.5 (PL 140: 956)

205. Fecisti periurium sciens et alium periurium ... in pane et aqua peniteas et non redimas.

Burch. 19.5 (PL 140: 956)

206. |p. 167| Promisisti meretrici aut adultere iuramento fidei ... malo quia scriptum iniusta vota fragenda sunt.

Burch. 19.5 (PL 140: 956)

207. Si iurasti per capillum Dei aut per caput eius ... vii. dies in pane et aqua peniteas.

Burch. 19.5 (PL 140: 956)

208. Si per celum aut per terram ... v. dies in pane et aqua peniteas.

1. celo T   Burch. 19.5 (PL 140: 956)

209. Si sacramento te obligasti ut ad pacem alicuius ... |p. 168| ... ceperit multitudinem peccatorum celeriter redi.

Burch. 19.5 (PL 140: 956–957)

210. Si definisti vel iuramento te offirmasti ... in iuramento in aliud crimen maius devertaris.

Burch. 19.5 (PL 140: 957)

211. SEQUITUR.

Furatus est aliquid de ecclesiastico infra ecclesia sive aurum ... |p. 169| ... reportatis sacris vii. carinas ieiunare debes.

Burch. 19.5 (PL 140: 957)

212. Si fregisti alicuius Christiani domum per noctem ... |p. 170| ... x. dies peniteas in pane et aqua.

Burch. 19.5 (PL 140: 957)

213. Si rapinam fecisti gravius debes penitere ... quando quod sibi dormiente valescente furatus est.

Burch. 19.5 (PL 140: 957)

214. Si fecisti furtum necessitatis causa sic dico ... et vi. ferias in pane et aqua peniteas.

Burch. 19.5 (PL 140: 957)

215. Mechatus es cum uxore alterius tu non habens uxorem ... carinam vocatur cum vii. sequentibus annis.

Burch. 19.5 (PL 140: 957)

216. |p. 171| Si mechatus tu uxoratus cum alterius uxore ... ecce aliud adulterium et numquam debes esse sine penitentia.

Burch. 19.5 (PL 140 : 957)

217. Si tu solus ab uxore cum femina vacantem ... si cum propria ancilla similiter paeniteas.

Burch. 19.5 (PL 140: 957–958)

218. Si dimisisti uxorem tuam et aliam duxisti ... |p. 172| ... quod Deus coniunxit homo non separet.

Burch. 19.5 (PL 140: 958)

219. Nulli liceat uxorem dimittere nisi causa fornicationis ... |p. 173| ... supra de uxore adulterius perpetrandi dictum est.

Burch. 19.5 (PL 140: 958)

220. Accepisti uxorem et non fecisti nuptias publice ... iii. quadragesimas per legitimas ferias penitere debes.

Burch. 19.5 (PL 140: 958)

221. Fecisti fornicationem cum sanctimonialibus seu sponsa Christi ... |p. 174| ... hos vi. ferias in pane et aqua observes.

Burch. 19.5 (PL 140: 958)

222. Si conrumpisti virginem et postea eadem eadem suscepisti uxorem ... post coruptionem uxorem ii. annos peniteas.

Burch. 19.5 (PL 140: 958)

223. Accepisti illam tibi uxorem quam alter sibi desponsatam ... carrinam vocat cum vii. sequentibus annis |p. 175| peniteas.

Burch. 19.5 (PL 140: 958)

224. Rapuisti uxorem tuam et vis sine volunta mulieris ... |p. 176| ... constitutum turbasti et violasti sine spe coniugii permaneas.

Burch. 19.5 (PL 140: 958–959)

225. Contigit tibi ut uxor tua te conscio et orante ... que tibi proposita sunt et sine spe coniugii permaneat.

Burch. 19.5 (PL 140: 959)

226. ALITER.

Accepisti uxorem cognatam tuam vel quam ... |pp. 177–178| ... peccato fueris penitentiam eius peccati nichil vadit.

Burch. 19.5 (PL 140: 959)

227. ALIUD.

Concubuisti cum uxore tua vel cum alia aliqua retro ... v. dies in pane et aqua peniteas.

Burch. 19.5 (PL 140: 959)

228. Iunxisti te uxori tue menstruo tempore ... |p. 179| ... cum ea his diebus dictis x. dies peniteas in pane et aqua.

Burch. 19.5 (PL 140: 959)

229. Concubuisti cum uxore tua postquam infans ... partum si fecisti x. dies peniteas.

Burch. 19.5 (PL 140: 959)

230. Concubuisti cum uxore post manifestam conceptionem v.dies peniteas.

Burch. 19.5 (PL 140: 959)

231. Concubuisti cum uxore tua die domenica iiii[or] dies penitere debes.

Burch. 19.5 (PL 140: 960)

232. Coinquinatus est cum uxore tua in quadragesima... penitere debes aut xxv. solidi in helimosinam daret.

Burch. 19.5 (PL 140: 959)

233. Si per ebrietatem venit xx. dies peniteas ... |p. 180| ... custodire si autem non custodisti xx. dies in pane et aqua peniteas.

Burch. 19.5 (PL 140: 959)

234. Fuisti in falso testimonio ita dico ut testimoniares ... et postea previ|p. 181|de ne tibi ulterius contingat.

Burch. 19.5 (PL 140: 959)

235. Violasti sepulchrum ita dico dum aliquem ... si fecisti v. duos annos per legitimas ferias peniteas.

Burch. 19.5 (PL 140: 960)

236. Consuluisti magos et domum tuam induxisti ... si fecisti ii. annos per legitimas ferias peniteas.

Burch. 19.5 (PL 140: 960)

237. Si observasti tradi|p. 182|tiones paganorum quasi hereditario ... omnia in nomine domini nostri Ihesu Christi facite.

Burch. 19.5 (PL 140: 960)

238. Observasti kalendas Januarias ritu paganorum vel aliquid ... |p. 183| ... ad illam vanitatem convertisti et apostata effectus es.

Burch. 19.5 (PL 140: 960–961)

239. Fecisti ligaturas et incantationes et illas varias ... |p. 184| ... si fecisti ii. annos per legitima(s) ferias peniteas.

Burch. 19.5 (PL 140: 961)

240. Interfuisti aut consentisti vanitatibus quas mulieres ... Si interfuisti aut consensisti xx. dies peniteas.

Burch. 19.5 (PL 140: 961)

241. |p. 185| Coluisti erbas medicinales cum aliis incantationibus ... si aliter fecisti x. dies peniteas.

Burch. 19.5 (PL 140: 961)

242. Venisti ad aliquem locum ad orandum nisi ad ecclesias ... iii. annos per legitimas ferias peniteas.

Burch. 19.5 (PL 140: 961)

243. Requisisti sortes in |p. 186| codicibus vel in tabulis ... presumant, si fecisti x. dies peniteas.

Burch. 19.5 (PL 140: 961)

244. Maledixisti patri vel matri tue vel flagellasti eos ... qui maledixerit patri suo vel matri morte moriatur.

Burch. 19.5 (PL 140: 962)

245. Tulisti aliquid de ecclesiastico thesauro si fecisti ... aut iii. annos per legitimas ferias peniteas.

Burch. 19.5 (PL 140: 962)

246. Seduxisti vel transmisisti vel vendidisti aliquem ... Si fecisti redde dannum et non annum peniteas.

Burch. 19.5 (PL 140: 962)

247. Coluisti ieiunium in quadragesima antequam vespertinum celebretur ... |p. 187| ... estimata vespertina ora completa oratio ieiunium solvat.

Burch. 19.5 (PL 140: 962)

248. Conte(m)psisti i(e)iunium indictum ad sanctam ecclesiam ... observare cum ceteris Christianis xx. dies peniteas in pane et aqua.

Burch. 19.5 (PL 140: 962)

249. Coluisti ieiunium quattuor temporum et non custodisti illud cum ceteris Christianis xl. dies paeniteas.

Burch. 19.5 (PL 140: 962)

250. Ieiunasti diem dominicum cum propter abstinentiam et religionem xx. dies in pane et aqua.

Burch. 19.5 (PL 140: 962)

251. |p. 188| Si non observasti diem letanie maioris ... xx. dies penitere debes in pane et aqua.

Burch. 19.5 (PL 140: 962)

252. Coegisti publice penitentem manducare et bibere ... si fecisti x. dies in pane et aqua peniteas.

Burch. 19.5 (PL 140: 962)

253. Contempsisti aliquem cum tu ieiunares qui ieiunare ... si fecisti v. dies in pane et aqua peniteas.

Burch. 19.5 (PL 140: 962)

254. Coluisti ieiunium in cena Domini et in sabbato ... si fecisti x. dies in pane et aqua peniteas.

Burch. 19.5 (PL 140: 962–963)

255. Habuisti in consuetudine ut plus comederes ... |p. 189| ... ne graventur in crapula et ebrietate.

Burch. 19.5 (PL 140: 963)

256. Bibisti umquam tantum ut per ebrietatem vomitum faceres, si fecisti xv. dies in pane et aqua peniteas.

Burch. 19.5 (PL 140: 963)

257. Inebriasti umquam per iactantiam ita dico ... si fecisti xxx. dies in pane et aqua peniteas.

Burch. 19.5 (PL 140: 963)

258. Fecisti vometum corporis et sanguinis Domini ... si fecisti xl. dies, id est carrinam unam peniteas.

Burch. 19.5 (PL 140: 963)

259. Si per nequitiam alios alium inebriasti xx. dies in pane et aqua peniteas.

Burch. 19.5 (PL 140: 963)

260. Neglexisti ut non acciperes corpus et sanguinem ... |p. 190| ... xx. dies penitere debes in pane et aqua.

Burch. 19.5 (PL 140: 963)

261. Disprevisti missam vel orationem coniugati ... videretur, si fecisti i. annum peniteas.

Burch. 19.5 (PL 140: 963)

262. Conspirasti vel cum aliis insidiatoribus contra episcopum ... si fecisti xl. dies in pane et aqua peniteas.

Burch. 19.5 (PL 140: 964)

263. Concubuisti cum sorore uxoris tue, si fe|p. 191|cisti ... vivatis iusta precepta sacerdotis penitentiam agite.

Burch. 19.5 (PL 140: 965)

264. Si absente uxore tua in lectum tuum ... debet affligi et in eternum coniugio debet privari.

Burch. 19.5 (PL 140: 965–966)

265. Fecisti fornicationem cum duabus sororibus et soror sororem ... |p. 192| ... usque ad mortem penitente et se ad coniugio abstineant.

Burch. 19.5 (PL 140: 966)

266. Fecisti fornicationem cum aliqua femina te scientem ... ad mortem et sine spe coniugii permaneant.

Burch. 19.5 (PL 140: 966)

267. Fecisti fornicationem cum filiastra tua, si fecisti nec matrem ... |p. 193| ... abuisti tecum non concubit nubaet in Domino si voluerit.

Burch. 19.5 (PL 140: 966)

268. Alias.

Fecisti fornicationem cum noverca tua, si fecisti neque tu ... pater autem tuus si voluerit aliam accipere potest.

Burch. 19.5 (PL 140: 966)

269. Fecisti fornicationem cum uxore fratris tui ... frater autem tuus si vult aliam accipiat.

Burch. 19.5 (PL 140: 966)

270. Fecisti fornicationem cum sponsa filii tui ... |p. 194| ... penitentia peracta sine spe coniugii permaneat.

Burch. 19.5 (PL 140: 966)

271. Fecisti fornicationem cum matre tua, si fecisti v. annis ... si se continere non vul(t) nubat in Domino.

Burch. 19.5 (PL 140: 966)

272. Fecisti fornicationem cum (co)matre tua, si fecisti separari ... pane et aqua cum vii. sequentibus annis peniteas.

Burch. 19.5 (PL 140: 966)

273. Fecisti fornicationem cum filiola tua spirituali ... |p. 195| ... carrinam vocant cum vii. sequentibus annis.

Burch. 19.5 (PL 140: 966–967)

274. Tenuisti filium tuum vel filiam tuam et filiastrum tuum... si se continere non potest nubat in Domino.

Burch. 19.5 (PL 140: 967)

275. Accepisti mulierem et habuisti eam per aliquod ... |pp. 196–197| ... separari potestis et illa nubat in Domino si vult.

Burch. 19.5 (PL 140: 967)

276. Fecisti fornicationem cum sorore tua, si fecisti x. annos ... si se continere non potest nubat in Domino.

Burch. 19.5 (PL 140: 967)

277. Fecisti fornicationem cum amita vel matertera ... |p. 198| ... nisi Christus a(l)iquam misericordiam tibi concedere voluerit.

Burch. 19.5 (PL 140: 967)

278. Fecisti fornicationem sicut sodomites fecerunt ita ut masculi terga ... scelum perpetrasti xv. penitere debes annos.

Burch. 19.5 (PL 140: 967–968)

279. Si cum masculo intra coxas ut quidam solent ... xl. dies in pane et aqua peniteas.

Burch. 19.5 (PL 140: 968)

280. |p. 199| Fecisti fornicationem ut quidam facere solent ita dico ut tu in manum ... xxx. dies in pane et aqua peniteas.

Burch. 19.5 (PL 140: 968)

281. Fecisti solum tecum fornicationem ut quidam facere solent ... proiceres x. dies in pane et aqua peniteas.

Burch. 19.5 (PL 140: 968)

282. Fecisti fornicationem ut quidam facere solent ut tuum virilem ... |p. 200| ... si fecisti xx. dies in pane et aqua peniteas.

Burch. 19.5 (PL 140: 968)

283. Dedisti obsculum alicui femine per inmundum desiderium ... polluisti, si fecisti i. diem in pane et aqua peniteas.

Burch. 19.5 (PL 140: 968)

284. Fecisti fornicationem contra naturam ut cum masculis ... penitere debes ut numquam sis sine penitentia.

Burch. 19.5 (PL 140: 968)

285. Si autem uxorem habuisti x. annis ... si in pueri|p. 201|tia tibi contigerat c. dies peniteas.

Burch. 19.5 (PL 140: 968)

286. Si autem servus est qui hoc fe(ce)rit ... ita peniteat ut illi qui in(g)enuus est.

2 inlenuum T Burch. 19.5 (PL 140: 968)

287. Comedisti scabiem corporalem pro aliqua sanitate ... vii. dies peniteas in pane et aqua.

Burch. 19.5 (PL 140: 968)

288. Comedisti morticinam id est animalia que a lupis ... si fecisti x. dies peniteas.

Burch. 19.5 (PL 140: 968)

289. |p. 202| Commedisti aves et animalia que in retibus ... x. dies peniteas in pane et aqua.

Burch. 19.5 (PL 140: 969)

290. Comedisti piscem qui mortuus in flumine inventus ... si fecisti iii. dies in pane et aqua peniteas.

Burch. 19.5 (PL 140: 969)

291. Fecisti falsitatem vel fraudem a(li)quam in mensuris ... x. dies in pane et aqua peniteas.

Burch. 19.5 (PL 140: 969)

292. Si obtrectasti turpitudinem tu coniugatus aliicuis ... non fuisti coniugatus unum diem peniteas.

Burch. 19.5 (PL 140: 969)

293. Lavasti te in balneo cum uxo|p. 203|re tua ... ii. dies in pane et aqua peniteas.

Burch. 19.5 (PL 140: 969)

294. Venerunt ad te ospites in tempore necessitatis ... v. dies in pane et aqua peniteas.

Burch. 19.5 (PL 140: 969)

295. Incendisti ecclesiam aut consensisti, si fecisti ... tuum pauperibus distribuerunt x. annis peniteas.

Burch. 19.5 (PL 140: 969)

296. Detenuisti oblationes mortuorum ita ut clericis ... voluisti, si fecisti unum annum peniteas.

Burch. 19.5 (PL 140: 969)

297. Celebrasti pentecostes, nata(lis) Domini in alio loco... si fecisti x. dies peniteas in pane et aqua.

Burch. 19.5 (PL 140: 969)

298. Habuisti aliquam communione |p. 204| cum excommunicato ... carrinam vocant cum vii. sequentibus annis.

Burch. 19.5 (PL 140: 969)

299. Detraxi(sti) vel retinuisti aliquid oblationibus quibus Deo ... |p. 205| ... vel consensisti xl. dies in pane et aqua debes penitere.

Burch. 19.5 (PL 140: 970)

300. Neglexisti decimam tuam dare quam Deus ipse ... et xx. dies in pane et aqua peniteas.

Burch. 19.5 (PL 140: 970)

301. Oppressisti paupere(s) qui tibi vicini erant ... |p. 206| ... et xxx. dies in pane et aqua peniteas.

Burch. 19.5 (PL 140: 970)

302. Fecisti quod quidam facere solent a sacerdote ... si fecisti iii. dies in pane et aqua peniteas.

Burch. 19.5 (PL 140: 970)

303. Accepisti corpus et sanguinem Domini post aliquam ... viatico fecisti x. dies in pane et aqua peniteas.

Burch. 19.5 (PL 140: 970)

304. Fecisti quod quidam facere solent dum ad ecclesiam ... si fecisti x. dies in pane et aqua peniteas.

Burch. 19.5 (PL 140: 970)

305. |p. 207| Vidisti pecatum fratris quod era(t) usque ad mortem ... si fecisti xxx. dies in pane et aqua peniteas.

Burch. 19.5 (PL 140: 970)

306. Fecisti tibi missam cantare et illa sancta ... si fecisti x. dies in pane et aqua peniteas.

Burch. 19.5 (PL 140: 970)

307. Fecisti quod quedam mulieres facere solent ut facerent quoddam molumen ... si fecisti iii. annos |p. 208| per legitimas ferias peniteas.

Burch. 19.5 (PL 140: 971–972)

308. Fecisti quod quedam mulieres facere solent ut iam dicto molumine ... facere fornicatione, si fecisti i. annum peniteas.

Burch. 19.5 (PL 140: 972)

309. Fecisti quod quedam mulieres facere solent quando libi(di)ne se vexante ... si fecisti iii. xl[me] per legitimas ferias peniteas.

Burch. 19.5 (PL 140: 972)

310. Fecisti quod quedam mulieres facere solent ut cum filio tuo ... si fecisti ii. annos per legitmas ferias peniteas.

Burch. 19.5 (PL 140: 972)

311. |p. 209| Fecisti quod quedam facere solent ut subcumberes ... cum vii. sequentibus annis peniteas et nunquam sis sine penitentia.

Burch. 19.5 (PL 140: 972)

312. Fecisti quod quedam mulieres facere solent que dum fornicantur et partus suo(s) ... si fecisti aut consensisti aut docuisti iii. annos per legitimas ferias peniteas.

Burch. 19.5 (PL 140: 972)

313. Set antiqua definitio usque ad exitum vite ... |p. 210| ... fornicaria causa et pro suis sceleribus celandi faciant.

Burch. 19.5 (PL 140: 972)

314. In concilio autem Hilderdensi de supradictis qui infantes suos ... omni tempore vite sue fletibus et umiliate insistant.

ILLERESINDUX T   Burch. 19.5 (PL 140: 972)

315. Donasti vel ostendisti alicui ut conceptuum ... |p. 211| ... post conceptum spiritum iii. annos penitere debes.

Burch. 19.5 (PL 140: 972)

316. ALIAS.

Interfecisti filium vel filiam voluntarie post partum ... penitere debes numquam esse sine penitentia.

Burch. 19.5 (PL 140: 972–973)

317. Neglexisti infantem tuum ut per tuam culpam ... per legitimas ferias penitere debes et numquam sis sine penitentia.

Burch. 19.5 (PL 140: 973)

318. Fecisti aliquem mortiferam et cum ea ... non perfecisti homicidium i. annum peniteas.

Burch. 19.5 (PL 140: 973)

319. Bibisti chrisma ad subvertendum iudicium Dei ... |p. 212| ... subvertere, si fecisti v. annos peniteas.

Burch. 19.5 (PL 140: 973)

320. IN CHRISTI NOMINE INCIPIT CELEBRATIO MISSE.

Dum quadam die resideret sanctissimus Papa Damascus in sede beati Petri apostoli intentio orta est ... |pp. 213–219| ... si cecum cecum duxerit ambo in foveam cadunt.

CELEBRATIONIS T   F. 3.212 (= C. 3.135, pp. 155–157)

321. DE HIS QUI (DE) GRADU ECCLESIASTICO OCCIDERE PRESUMPSERIT.

Synodus Nicaena a ccc^{torum} et x. et viii. episcopis sub Constantino Augusto peracta. Qui episcopum a(u)t presbiterum vel diaconum occiderit ad iudicandum regi dimittendus est ... |p. 220| ... ex (h)is et residuos vii. ut scriptum est peniteat.

DE HIS] INCIPIT CONCILIIS T   GRADO T   episcoporum T   dimittendum T
V. 4.108 (f. 188va) (= C. 4.63.3, p. 215)

322. UNDE SUPRA. IUDICIUM THEODORI.

Si quis occiderit episcopum vel presbiterum sive diaconum regis est dimittendus. Qui vero monachum vel clericum occiderit ... vel x. seu xii. annis peniteat.

dimittendum T   V. 4.107.2 (f. 188va) (= C. 3.63.2, p. 215)

323. DE HOMICIDIO CLERICORUM. IUDICIO COMMEANI.

Si quis episcopum homicidium fecerit xv. annis peniteat ... |p. 221| ... in exitu vite sue sacris corporis recipiat quanto magis ordines clericorum.

V. 4.109.1 (f. 188vb) (= C. 4.64.1, pp. 315 f.)

324. GREGORIUS.

Si quid clericus homicidium fecerit vii. annis peniteat |p. 222| ex his iii. annis exsul fiat.

V. 4.109.2 (f. 189ra) (= C. 4.64.1, p. 316)

325. GREGORIUS.

Qui patrem vel matrem vel sororem aut fratrem sive filium seu compatrem aut filium de sacro lavacro etiam seniorem proprium et alio(s) similes voluntarie occiderit ... in monasterio usque·ad mortem cum luctu peniteat.

V. 4.110 (f. 189ra) (= C. 4.65, p. 216)

326. DE VIRO QUI UXOREM SUAM CUM CAUSA VEL SINE CAUSA OCCIDERIT.

Placuit sacro et magno Calcedones Concilio ubi ducenti xxx. sacerdotes sub Marciano principe affuerunt ut si quis vir uxorem suam sine causa occiderit ... |p. 223| ... hoc contigit v. annos iudicio sacerdotis peniteat.

in Concilio T   V. 4.112.1 (f. 189rb) (= C. 4.81, p. 219)

327. DE QUO SUPRA.

Et si qua mulier virum suum quacumque diabolica arte vel fraude occiderit ... et sacramentum Christi non nisi ad mortis exitum percipiat.

percipiant T   V. 4.112.2 (f. 189rb) (= C. 4.81, p. 219)

328. DE VII GENERIBUS NOLENTIBUS HOMICIDIORUM. CONCILIUM QUOD SUPRA.

Septem genera sunt nolentia homicidiorum: i. cum quis aut in preda ... |pp. 224–226| ... nolente tamen difficile sine neglegentia hoc invenitur.

NOLENTIA T SUPRA] FECIT T V. 4.113 (f. 189va) (= C. 4.80, p. 219)

329. DE HIS QUI SPONTE HOMICIDIUM COMMISERI(N)T. CONCILIO ANCIRANO.

Qu(i) voluntarie homicidium feceri(n)t penitentie quidem iugiter se submitta(n)t; perfectionem vero circa vite exitum consequantur.

V. 4.114.2 (f. 190ra) (= C. 4.69.1, p. 216)

330. DE HOMICIDIO VOLUNTARIE VEL CAUSA. CONCILIO AGATENSE.

Si quis voluntarie homicidium fecerit ad ianuam ecclesie catholice semper subiaceat ... |p. 227| ... prior canon vii. annis penitere secundus canon v. mandavit.

secundum T V. 4.114.3 (f. 190ra) (= C. 4.69.2, p. 216)

331. DE HOMICIDIO LAICORUM. GREGORIUS.

Si laicus occiderit alterum laicum xl. dies abstineat se ab ecclesia ... si in prelio aut in conventu xl. dies.

V. 4.115.2 (f. 190rb) (= C. 4.71.2, p. 217)

332. DE DIVERSIS HOMICIDIIS. IUDICIUM THEODORI.

Qui occiderit hominem per rixam sine meditatione ... |pp. 228–229|... quis est moriturus. Hi tales xl. dies peniteant.

HOMICIDIUM T V. 4.115.3 (f. 190rb) (C. 4.71.1, pp. 216–217)

333. DE DIVERSIS HOMICIDIIS SIVE VOLUNTARIE SIVE NOLENS.

Sancta Sinodus cl. patribus sub Theodosio seniorem Constantinopoli congregata epilogus breviter degustus ... |pp. 230–231| ... socerum suum aut socrum x. annis peniteat.

V. 4.115.7 (f. 190va) (= C. 4.79, p. 218)

334. Gravius est industria quam per infirmitate(m) pec(c)are. Sic semper provindendum est peritissimi(s) sacerdotibus, quod si de ordine clericorum de (h)is sevissimis malis aliquid ammiserit ... |p. 232| ... . unde laicus vii., subdiaconus x., diaconus et monachus xii., presbiter xiii., episcopus xv., et cetera similia.

industriam T V. 4.115.22 (f. 191ra) (= C. 4.79, pp. 218–219)

335. ALITER.

Caveat ante omnia sacerdos ne de his qui ei confitentur peccata sua alicui recitet quod ei confessus est ... omnibus diebus vite sue ignominiosus peregrinando peniteat.

quod]qui T V. 4.69.2 (f. 180vb) (= C. 4.41.3, p. 207)

336. BASILIUS EPISCOPUS.

Si quis sacerdos palam fecerit et secretum penitentie usurpaverit ... in cunctum populum deponatur et diebus vite sue inter eos peregrinando finiat.

cunctus populus T V. 4.69.3 (f. 181ra) (= C. 4.41.4, p. 208)

337. DE HIS QUI AD MERCEDEM IEIUNABITUR.

Synodus Romana. Si quis ad mercedem ieiunaverit si per ignoran|p. 233| tia(m) ... si autem per industriam hoc presumitur anathematizetur.

HEIS T V. 4.78 (f. 184ra) (= C. 4.47.2, p. 209)

338. DE HIS QUI SERVOS SUO(S) (NECANT) EXTRA IUDICIUM. CONCILIO AGATENSE.

Si quis servum proprium sine conscientia iudicis occiderit ... vel penitentie bienni reatum sanguinis emundavit.

V. 4.116 (f. 191rb)(= C. 4.68.1, p. 216)

339. SI DOMINA PER ZELUM ANCILLAM OCCIDERIT. EX CONCILIO LIBERITANO.

Si qua femina furore zeli accensa flagellis verberaverit ancillam suam ... infra tempore constituta fuerit infirmata accipiat communionem.

EXTRA T cumfra T V. 4.117.1 (f. 191rb) (= C. 4.68.2, p. 216)

340. DE MALEFICIIS.

Sinodus (An)cyrana. Si quis per maleficia aliquem hominem ... |p. 234| ... dilexerit set non affectaverit iiii. annis peniteat.

MAFICIIS T   V. 4.117.2 (f. 191rb) (= C. 4.72.1, p. 217)

341. DE HIS QUI SIBI MORTEM INFERUNT VEL PRO SUIS SCELERIBUS PUNIUNTUR. CONCILIO BRACA(RE)NISE.

Placuit ut hi qui sibi ipsis aut per ferrum aut per venenum ... |p. 235| ... excepto hi qui per infirmitatem a demonibus arripiuntur.

his T   V. 4.119.1 (f. 191va) (= C. 4.73, p. 217)

342. DE HIS QUI VEXATI SUNT A DIABOLO FORTE SE IPSO(S) INTERFICIUNT.

Synodus Romana. Si quis vexatus a diabolo et nesciens semetipsum occidit licet adorare pro eo.

V. 4.119.2 (f. 191va) (= C. 4.74, p. 217)

343. DE HOMICIDIO (QUOD) IN CONGREGATIO(NE) MONACHORUM IUDICETUR. CONCILIO CARTAGINENSE.

Si quis homicidium perpetraverit iudicio episcopi est si religiosus fuerit ... fiat vite aliene et quia non potest cecum caeco ducatum prebere.

HOMICIDIUM T   IUDICENTUR T   CATANENSE T   iudicium T
V. 4.121 (f. 191vb) (= C. 4.76.2, pp. 217 f.)

344. DE TRADITORIBUS.

Synodus Romana. Si alium quis homo in manu(s) inimici tradiderit ... |p. 236| ... etiamsi traditus nutu Dei ab inimicis evaserit.

V. 4.123.1 (f.192rb) (= C. 4.82.1, p. 219 (Titulus), p. 220 (Textus in margine).

345. ITE(M). UNDE SUPRA.

Si quis castellum aut alicuius municipium in manibus inimicorum ... |p. 237| ... dampnationem sustineat cum suis omnibus sequacibus.

V. 4.123.2 (f. 192rb) (= C. 4.82.2, p. 220)

346. DE OBPRESSIS INFANTIBUS. GREGORIUS PAPA.

Si qua fidelis mulier oppresserit per neglegentiam infantem in quo mortuus fuerit ... circa neglectum suum iudicio sacerdotis peniteat.

V. 4.125 (f. 192va) (= C. 4.84.1, p. 220)

347. DE MULIERE QUE INFANTEM SUUM MORTUUM INVENERIT. IUDICIUM COMMEANI.

Si qua mulier invenerit iusta se infantem suum mortuum ... |p. 238| ... si vero baptizatus xl. dies peniteat.

QUI T V. 4.126 (f. 192va) (= C. 4.84.3, p. 220)

348. AUGUSTINUS.

Que mulier aut laborat ut nec concipiat aut partum suum disperdet aut filium suum necat, si quis consentietes ei in hoc peccatum fuerit, x. annis districte peniteat.

V. 4.129.2 (f. 193ra) (= C. 4.85.4, pp. 220 f.)

349. Item.

Nulla mu(li)er potionem accipiat aut conceptum occidat ... |p. 239| ... sciat se esse cum parricidis causa(m) reddituram.

sciat]fiat T; redditurας T V. 4.129.3 (f. 193ra) (= C. 4.85.4, p. 221)

350. Ite(m).

Nulla(s) potiones diabolica(s) debent mulieres accipere per quas non possi(n)t concipere ... debuerit tantorum homicidiorum ream se esse cognoverit.

concipere]accipere T V. 4.129.4 (f. 193ra) (= C. 4.85.4, p. 221)

351. DE HIS QUI PARTUS SUO(S) INTERIM(UN)T. CONCILIO ANCIRANO.

Si qua mulier fornicaverit et infantem qui exinde fuerit natus occiderit ... conscias sce|p. 240|leriam ipsarum x. annos agere penitentiam iudicamus.

V. 4.131 (f. 193rb) (= C. 4.86, p. 221)

352. DE MULIERE QUE OCCI(DIT) FILIUM SUUM. CONCILIO ANCIRANO.

Mulier que concepit et occidit filium suum in ute(ro) ante xl. dies ... sine baptismo vii. annorum addatur penitentia.

V. 4.133 (f. 193va) (= C. 4.86.3, p. 221)

353. DE HIS QUI CONCEPTUM MULIERIS DECEP(ER)I(N)T. ANCIRANO.

Si quis conceptum mulieris deceperit si ante x(l). dies ... si autem plus xl. dies ut homicida peniteat.

DECEPIT T quis] qua T V. 4.134 (f. 193vb) (= C. 4.87, p. 221)

354. DE PATRE ET MATRE SI NATUM FILIUM NECAVERIT. IUDICIUM CANONUM.

Pater aut mater scisciens voluntarie necat filium suum ante baptismum xv. annis peniteat ... eruditi sacerdotis fiat si vero post baptismum secundum modum |p. 241| culpe previdеant et vires hominis.

PATREM T eruditis T V. 4.135 (f. 193vb) (= C. 4.88, p. 221)

355. DE HIS QUI ECCLESIE PER INIQUA(M) INTENTIONEM VIOLA(TO)RES EXTITERI(N)T.

Sinodus Effesina. Primum (a) ccc[torum]xviii episcopis sub iuniore Theodosio Agusto edita. Si quis Dei ecclesie per iniquam intentionem violatores existeri(n)t ... templum Dei violaverit disperdet illum Deus.

ep(iscop)orum T; 4 que T V. 4.136 (f. 194ra) (C. non invenitur)

356. (DE HIS QUI ECCLESIAS DEI) PER MALAM INTENTIONEM DISSIPAVERI(N)T.

Placuit sancte et magne Synodo Nicene que (a) ccc et xviii. episcopi(s) sub Constantino Augusto est peracta u(t) Si quis ecclesiam Dei per odium vel a(li)qua(m) intentionem ... |p. 242| ... orationibus se redima sicut sancta Sinodus Nicena statuit.

quae T V. 4.137 (f. 194ra) (C. non invenitur)

357. DE HIS QUI PER SUE TIRANNIDIS POTENTIA(M) CONTRA DOMINI ATQUE SANCTE ECCLESIE CUIUS(LI)BET GRADUM MITTERE MANUS AUSI FUERINT. EX CONCILIO LAODICENSE.

Si quis Dei sancteque ecclesie extiterit conte(m)ptor ... |pp. 243–244| ... dampnatione sustineat penam cum suis omnibus.

AUSUS FUERIT T   V. 4.139.3 (f. 195ra) (= C. 4.114.2, p. 229)

358. DE HIS QUI MEMBRA SUA ABSCIDUNT. IUDICIA CANONICUM.

Si quis quodlibet membrum precipue tamen |p. 245| virilia ... omnimodis inrevocabiliter submoveantur, si laicus fuerit iii. annis.

quae qualibet T   V. 4.140 (f. 195va) (= C. 4.89.1, p. 222)

359. DE HIS QUI ACCUSANT NEC PROBANT. GREGORIUS.

Si quis episcopum vel presbiterum aut diaconum falsis criminibus appetierit ... in finem danda(m) ei esse communionem iudicamus.

quis] quae T   V. 4.149 (f. 196rb) (= C. 4.93.3, p. 223)

360. DE FALSO TESTIMONIO. IUDICIO COMEANI.

Si quis falsum testimonium dixerit, si episcopus fuerit vii. annis ... antequam studens inquirat ii. annis peniteat.

quis] quae T   V. 4.152 (f. 196va) (= C. 4.94.2, p. 223)

361. DE DA(M)PNANDIS CLERICIS PER TEMERITATEM. CONCILIO TARACONENSE.

Ut non da(m)pnetur episcopus in sancta sinodo ... |p. 246| nec presbiter nisi xliiii., nec diaconus nisi xxxvii. testimonia.

F. 3.279; V. 3.222.2 (f. 147ra) (= C. 3.183.1, p.168)

362. DE HIS QUI PATRI VEL MATRI PER IRACUNDIA(M) MANUM EREX(E)RI(N)T. CONCILIUM TARACONENSE.

Si quis super patrem suum vel matrem iracundia manum erexerit ... vel matrem in Christo. Si quis patrem aut matrem in verbo exhonoraverit iii. annis peniteat.

MANUUM T   quis] que   V. 4.185 (f. 201va) (cf C. 4.111.2, p. 228)

363. DE FURTO ECCLESIE QUOD SACRILEGIUM DICITUR. GREGORIUS.

Sacrilegium dicitur id est sacr(ar)um rerum furtum ... |p. 247| ... furis pensandum est qualiter valeat corrigi.

QUI T Sacrilegius T V. 4.207 (f. 204rb) (= C. 4.124.3, p. 233)

364. DE FURTO CAPITALI. GREGORIUS.

Si quis furtum capitale commiserit id est aurum argentum ... |p. 248| aliquid furti faciens vii. dies peniteat.

V. 4.210 (f. 204vb) (= C. 4.125.1, p. 233)

365. DE HIS QUI FURT(IV)U(M)COMED(UNT). GREGORIUS.

Quicumque furt(iv)u(m)comederit etsi pauper est ... dictum est si vero maior addatur.

V. 4.213 (f. 205ra) (= C. 4.127.1, p. 234)

366. DE HOMINE QUI SINE CA(U)SA SPOLIAVERIT.

Sinodus Hibernensis. Si quis homines gratis expoliaverit in via ... censura reconciliaverit cum fratre su(o) quem expoliaverit.

que T V. 4.225 (f. 206va) (= C. 4.135, p. 235)

367. DE PERIURIO. IUDICIUM GREGORII.

Si quis in altare ubi reliquie habentur ... |p. 249| ... si tamen per consensum iii. peniteat.

quis]que T; anltare T V. 4.243 (f. 209rb) (= C. 4.144, p. 239)

368. DE PERIURIO COACTO.

Si quis coactus invitus pro qualibet causa necessitatis se periuraverit iii. annis peniteat.

COACTUM T em. que T V. 4.244 (f. 209va) (= C. 4.145, p. 239)

369. DE PERIURIO IN MANU SACERDOTIS AUT IN CRUCE CONSECRATA.

Si quis in manu episcopi vel presbiteri aut in cruce consecrata se periuraverit secundum antiquam deffinitionem v. annis peniteat.

AUTEM T que T V. 4.245 (f. 209va) (= C. 4.146.1, p. 239)

370. DE SACRIFICII VOMITU. IUDICIUM CANONUM.

Si quis sacrificium evomuerit xl. dies seu amplius... |p. 250| ... si post media(m) noctem ii., si post matutinum unum superpositionem.

DE SACRIFICIO VOMITUM T que T

V. 4.326 (f. 223va) (= C. 4.184.3, p. 353 [in added section at end of MS])

371. IUDICIUM CANONICUM.

Si quis sacerdos missa(s) celebraverit et non communicaverit i. anno peniteat.

que T V. 4.237.2 (f. 232vb) (= C. 4.185.2, p. 353)

372. DE QUADRAGESIMIS ET IEIUNIIS IN ANNO CONSTITUTIS. IUDICIO CANONICO.

Legitime quadragesime tres sunt a populi(s) constitute ... |p. 251| ... versus fueri vita vivet et non morietur.

QUADRAGESIMA T IEIUNIA T CONSTITUTA T tria T constituta T

V. 4.335.1 (f. 225rb) (cf. C. 4.[188.1], p.355)

373. ITEM ALIUS.

Mense primo ebdomada prima iiii[ta]. et vi. feria ... festivitatesque sanctis patribus per singulos annos constitute sunt.

V. 4.335.1.8 (f. 225va) (= C. 4.[188.1], p. 355)

374. DE EO QUOD IEIUNANDUM EST IIII. ET VI. FERIIS ET SINE ERRORE.

Ista sancta ieiunia sane legitima, id est iiii[ta] et vi. feria... |p. 252| ... traentem tradere salvatorem vel crucifigentibus crucifigere.

QUI T V.4.354 (f. 227vb) (= C. 4.193.2, p. 359)

375. GREGORIUS.

Si quis die dominico per neglegentiam ieiunaverit ... si illud iteraverit xl. dies peniteat.

quid T illum T V. 4.373.2 (f. 230ra) (= C. 4.196.1, p. 361)

376. PATERIUS.

Qui in xl. ieiunium solvit si tamen ieiunare valet pro i. die vii. dies peniteat.

V. 4.374 (f. 230ra) (= C. 4.196.2, p. 361)

377. DE FACILE FORNICATIONE. GREGORIUS.

Si quis pontifex faciens facile(m) fornicatione(m) ... |p. 253| ... post acta(m) penitentiam reconcilietur ad communionem.

que T F. 2.64 (= C. 2.31.1, p. 84)

378. DE GRAVE FORNICATIONE. IUDICIO COMMEANI.

Si quis cum Deo sacrata vel uxore alterius ... nam et ad sacerdotii gradus numquam accedat.

F. 2.65 (= C. 2.31.2, pp. 84 f.)

379. DE DIVERSIS FORNICATIONIBUS VITIORUM. IUDICIO COMMEANI.

Si obsculatus (est) episcopus per desiderium mulierem ... |pp. 254–255| ... et a sacerdotio priventur, clericus et laicus v. vel quattuor annis peniteat.

F. 2.66 (= C. 2.32, p. 85)

380. EX CONCILIO LAODICENSE.

Qui venerit in secunda(s) nuptias penitentiam ... si enim v. difficile ut acta penitentia inveniatur.

V. 5.31.2 (f. 259rb) (= C. 23.2, p. 277)

381. INSTITUTA PATRUM REGULA.

Si quis legitimam uxorem dimiserit et acceperit aliam ... manducet set excommunicati a Christianis fia(n)t.

V. 5.167.2 (f. 293vb) (= C. 5.84.2, p. 311)

382. DE FEMINIS QUE CONSCIIS MARITI(S) SE ADULTERANT. CONCILIO LIBERITANO.

Si qua femina conscio marito fuerit adulterata ... habitare cum ea placuit nec in finem danda(m) ei esse <communionem>.

QUI T ADULTERATA T quis T adulteratam T e(ss)et T
V. 5.157 (f. 291ra) (= C. 5.79.2, p. 308)

Initia canonum

Index of Subjects